SELECT SERMONS

By D. L. MOODY

_____

"PREACH THE WORD"

Fredonia Books
Amsterdam, The Netherlands

Select Sermons

by
D. L. Moody

ISBN: 1-58963-325-3

Copyright © 2001 by Fredonia Books

Reprinted from the 1897 edition

Fredonia Books
Amsterdam, The Netherlands
http://www.fredoniabooks.com

Preface.

In compliance with the wish of many friends I have consented to the publication of the following Addresses.

I deeply feel how partially and insufficiently the Glorious Gospel of the blessed God is represented in them, but I lay them at the Master's feet. praying, and asking all my Christian friends to pray, that they may be the means in their printed form of winning more souls to Christ then they have been when spoken.

D. L. Moody.

CONTENTS

I.

WHERE ART THOU?

GENESIS III, 9.

The very first thing that happened after the news reached heaven of the fall of man, was that God came straight down to seek out the lost one. As He walks through the garden in the cool of the day, you can hear Him calling—

"Adam! Adam! *Where art thou?*"

It is the voice of grace, of mercy, and of love. Adam ought to have taken the seeker's place, for he was the transgressor. He had fallen, and he ought to have gone up and down Eden crying,

"My God! my God! where art *Thou?*"

But God left heaven to grope through the dark world for the rebel who had fallen—not to hurl him from the face of the earth, but to plan for him an escape from the misery of his sin. And He finds him—where? Hiding from his Creator among the bushes of the garden.

The moment a man is out of communion with God, even the professed child of God, he wants to hide away from Him. When God left Adam in the garden, he was in communion with his Creator, and God talked with him; but now he has fallen, he has no desire to see his Creator, he has lost communion with his God. He cannot bear to see Him, even to think of Him, and he runs to hide from God. But to his hiding place his Maker follows him. "Where art thou, Adam? Where art thou?"

Six thousand years have passed away, and this text has come rolling down the ages. I doubt whether there has been one of Adam's sons who has not heard it at some period or other of his life—sometimes in the midnight hour stealing over him—"Where am I? Who am I? Where am I going? and what is going to be the end of this?" I think it is well for a man to pause and ask himself those questions. I would have you ask it, little boy; and you, little girl; and you, old man with locks turning grey, and eyes growing dim, and natural force abating—you who will soon be in another world. I do not ask you where you are in the sight of your neighbors; I do not ask you where you are in the sight of your friends; I do not ask you where you are in the sight of the community in which you live. It is of very little account where we are in the sight of one another, it is of very little account what men think of us; but it is of vast importance what *God* thinks of us.

It is of vast importance to know where men are in the sight of God; and that is the question now. Am I in communion with my Creator, or out of communion? If I am out of communion, there is no peace, no joy, no happiness. No man on the face of the earth who is out of communion with his Creator ever knows what peace, and joy, and happiness, and true comfort are. He is a foreigner to it. But when we are in communion with God, there is light all around our path.

So ask yourself this question. Do not think I am addressing your neighbor, but remember I am trying to speak to you, as if you were alone. It was the first question put to man after his fall, and it was a very small audience God had—Adam and his wife. But God was the preacher; and although they tried to hide, the words came home to them. Let them come home to you now. You may think that your life is hid, that God does not know anything about you; but He knows our lives a great deal better than we do, and His eye has been upon us from our earliest childhood until now.

"Where art thou?" I should like to divide my audience into three classes—the professed Christians, the Backsliders, and the Ungodly.

I.

First, I would like to ask the professors this question —or rather let God ask it—Where art thou? What is your position in the church, and among your circle of acquaintances? Do your friends know you to be out= and=out on the Lord's side? You may have been a professing Christian for twenty years, perhaps thirty, perhaps forty years. Well, where are you to=night? Are you making progress toward heaven? And can you give a reason for the hope that is within you? Suppose I were to ask those here who are really Christians to rise, would you be ashamed to stand up? Suppose I should ask every professed child of God here: " If you should be cut down by the hand of death, have you *good* reason to believe you would be saved?" Would you be willing to stand up before God and man, and say that you have good reason to believe you have passed from death unto life? Or would you be ashamed? Let your mind run back over the past years: would it be consistent for *you* to say, "I am a Christian"; and would your life correspond with your profession? It is not what we say so much as how we live. Actions speak louder than words. Do your shopmates know you are a Christian? Does your family know? Do they know you to be out=and=out on the Lord's side?

Let every professed Christian ask, Where am I in the sight of God? Is my heart loyal to the King of heaven? Is my life here as it should be in the community I live in? Am I a light in this dark world? Christ says, "Ye are my witnesses." Christ was the Light of the world, and the world would not have the true Light. The world rose up and put out the Light, and now Christ says, "I leave *you* down here to testify of me. I leave you down here as my witnesses." That is what the apostle meant when he said that Christians are to be living epistles, known and read of all men. Am I then standing up for Jesus as I should in this dark world? If a man is for God let him say so. If a man is for God, let him come out and be on God's side; and if he is for the world, let him be in the world. This serving God and the world at the same time—this being on both sides at the same time—is the curse of Christianity to=day. It retards its progress more than any other thing. "If any man will come after me, let him deny himself, and take up his cross *daily* and follow me."

I have heard of a great many people who think that if they are united to the church, and have made one profession, that will do for all the rest of their days. But there is a cross for every one of us *daily*. Oh, child of God, where are you? If God should appear to you to=

night in your bedroom and put the question, what would be your answer? Could you say, "Lord, I am serving Thee with my whole heart and strength; I am improving my talents and preparing for the kingdom to come"?

When I was in England in 1867, there was a merchant who came over from Dublin, and was talking with a business man in London; and as I happened to look in, he introduced me to the man from Dublin. Alluding to me, the latter said to the former.

"Is this young man all O O?"

Said the London man, "What do you mean by O O?"

"*Is he Out-and-Out for Christ?*"

I tell you it burned down into my soul. It means a good deal to be O O for Christ; but that is what all Christians ought to be, and their influence would be felt on the world very soon if men who are on the Lord's side would come out and take their stand, and lift up their voices in season and out of season.

As I have said, there are a great many in the church who make one profession, and that is about all you hear of them. When they come to die you have to go and hunt up some musty old church records, to know whether they were Christians or not. God won't do that. I have an idea that when Daniel died, all the men in Babylon knew whom he served. There was no need for them to hunt up old books. His life told his story. What we want is men with a little courage to stand up for Christ. When Christianity wakes up, and every child that belongs to the Lord is willing to speak for Him, is willing to work for Him, and (if need be) willing to die for Him, then Christianity will advance, and we shall see the work of the Lord prosper.

There is one thing which I fear more than anything else, and that is the dead, cold formalism of the Church of God. Talk about *isms!* Put them all together, and I do not fear them so much as dead, cold formalism. Talk about *false isms!* There is none so dangerous as this dead, cold formalism, which has come right into the heart of the Church. There are so many of us sleeping and slumbering while souls all around are perishing. I believe honestly that we professed Christians are all half-asleep. Some of us are beginning to rub our eyes and to get them half-opened, but as a whole we are asleep.

Some time ago a little story that made a great impression upon me as a father, went the round of the secular press. A father took his little child out into the field one Sabbath, and, it being a hot day, he lay down under a beautiful shady tree. The little child ran about gathering wild flowers and little blades of grass, and coming to its father and saying, "Pretty! pretty!" At last the father fell asleep, and while he was sleeping the little child wandered away. When he awoke, his first thought was, "Where is my child?" He looked all around, but he could not see him. He shouted at the top of his voice, but all he heard was the echo of his own voice. Running to a little hill, he looked around and shouted again. No response! Then going to a precipice at some distance, he looked down, and there upon the rocks and briars he saw the mangled form of his loved child. He rushed to the spot, took up the lifeless corpse and hugged it to his bosom, and accused himself of being the murderer of his child. While he was sleeping his child had wandered over the precipice.

I thought as I read that, what a picture of the church

of God! How many fathers and mothers, how many Christian men, are now sleeping while their children wander over the terrible precipice right into the bottomless pit of hell! Father, where is your boy to-night? It may be in some saloon; it may be reeling through the streets; it may be pressing onwards to a drunkard's grave. Mother, where is your son? Is he spending his evening drinking away his soul—everything that is dear and sacred to him? Do you know where your boy is? Father, you have been a professed Christian for forty years; where are your children to-night? Have you lived so godly and so Christlike a life that you can say, Follow me as I have followed Christ? Are your children walking in wisdom? are they on their way to glory? have they been gathered into the fold of Christ? are their names written in the Lamb's Book of Life? How many fathers and mothers to-day would be able to answer yes? Did you ever stop to think that you are to blame, that you have not been faithful to your children? Depend upon it, as long as the church is living so much like the world, we cannot expect our children to be brought into the fold.

Come, O Lord, and wake up every mother, and may everyone of us who are parents feel the worth of the souls of the children that God has given us! May they never bring our grey hairs with sorrow to the grave, but may they become a blessing to the church and to the world!

Not long ago the only daughter of a wealthy friend of mine sickened and died. The father and mother stood by her dying bed. He had spent all his time in accumulating wealth for her. She had been introduced into gay and fashionable society: but she had been taught

nothing of Christ. As she came to the brink of the
river of death, she said, "Won't you help me? it is very
dark, and the stream is bitterly cold." They wrung
their hands in grief, but could do nothing for her; and
the poor girl died in darkness and despair. What was
their wealth to them then? And yet, mothers and
fathers are doing the very same thing to-day, by ignor-
ing the work God has given you to do. I beseech you,
each one of you, begin to labor now for the souls of
your children!

Some time ago a young man lay dying, and his mother
thought he was a Christian. One day, passing the door
of his room, she heard him say, "Lost! lost! lost!"
The mother ran into the room and cried, "My boy, is it
possible you have lost your hope in Christ, now you are
dying?" "No, mother, it is not that. I have a hope
beyond the grave, but I have lost my life. I have lived
twenty-four years, and have done nothing for the Son
of God, and now I am dying. My life has been spent
for myself. I have lived for this world, and now, while
I am dying, I have given myself to Christ; but my life
is lost."

Would it not be said of many of us, if we should be
cut down, that our lives have been almost a failure—
perhaps entirely a failure as far as leading any one else
to Christ is concerned? Young lady! are you working
for the Son of God? Are you trying to win some soul
to Christ? Have you tried to get some friend or companion to have her name written in the Book of Life?
Or would you say, "Lost! lost! long years have rolled
away since I became a child of God, and I have never
had the privilege of leading one soul to Christ"? If
there is one professed child of God who has never had

the joy of leading even one soul into the kingdom of God, oh! let him begin at once. There is no greater privilege on earth.

Oh, may God wake up the Church! Let us trim our lights, and go forth and work for the kingdom of His Son.

II.

Now, secondly, let me talk a little while to those who have gone back into the world—to backsliders.

It may be you went to some great city a few years ago a professed Christian. You were member of a church once, and a teacher in the Sabbath-school, perhaps; but when you went among strangers you thought you would just wait a little—perhaps take a class by and by. So you gave up teaching in the Sunday-school; you gave up all work for Christ. Then in your new church you did not receive the attention or the warm welcome that you expected, and you got into the habit of staying away. You have gone so far now that you are found in the theater, perhaps, and the companion or blasphemers and drunkards.

Perhaps I am speaking now to some one who has been away from his Father's house for many years. Come, now, backslider, tell me—are you happy? Have you had one happy hour since you left Christ? Does the world satisfy you, or those husks that you have got in the far country? I have traveled a good deal, but I never found a happy backslider in my life. I never knew a man who was really born of God that ever could find the world satisfy him afterwards. Do you think the prodigal son was satisfied in that foreign country? Ask the prodigals to-day if they are truly happy. You know they are not. "There is no peace, saith my God, to the wicked." There is no joy for man in rebellion against his Creator. Supposing he has tasted the heavenly gift, has been in communion with God, has had sweet fellowship with the King of heaven and pleasant hours of service for the Master, but has backslidden, is it possible that he can be happy? If he is, it is good evidence he was never really converted. If a man has been born again, and has received the heavenly nature, this world can never satisfy the cravings of his nature.

Oh, backslider, I pity you! But I want to tell you that the Lord Jesus pities you a good deal more than any one else can. He knows how bitter your life is. He knows how dark your life is. He wants you to come home. Oh, backslider, come home now! I have a loving message from your Father. He wants you, and calls you back. " Come home, oh wanderer: return from the dark mountains of sin." Return and your Father will give you a warm welcome.

I know that the devil has told you that God won't have anything to do with you, because you have wandered away. If that were true, there would be very few men in heaven. David backslid. Abraham and Jacob turned away from God. I do not believe there is a saint in heaven but at some time of his life with his heart he backslid from God. Perhaps not in his outward life, but in his heart. The prodigal's heart got into the far country before his body got there.

Backslider! come home. Your Father does not want you to stay away. Think you the prodigal's father was not anxious for him to come home all those long years he was away? Every year the father was looking and longing for him to return. So God wants you to come home. I do not care how far you have wandered away; the great Shepherd will receive you back into the fold now. Did you ever hear of a backslider coming home and God not willing to receive him? I have heard of earthly fathers and mothers not being willing to receive back their sons; but I defy any man to say he ever knew a really honest backslider want to get home, but God was willing to take him in.

A number of years ago, before any railway came into Chicago, they used to bring in the grain from the western prairies in wagons for hundreds of miles, so as to have it shipped off by the lakes. There was a father who had a large farm out there, and who used to preach the gospel as well as attend to his farm. One day, when church business engaged him, he sent his son to Chicago with grain. He waited and waited for his boy to return, but he did not come home. At last he could wait no longer, so he saddled his horse and rode to the place where his son had sold the grain. He found that he had been there and got the money for the grain. Then he began to fear that his boy had been murdered and robbed. At last, with the aid of a detective, he tracked him to a gambling den, where he found that he had gambled away the whole of his money. In hopes of winning it back again, he had then sold the team and lost that money too. He had fallen among thieves, and like the man who was going to Jericho, they stripped him, and then cared no more about him. What could he do? He was ashamed to go home and meet his father, and he fled. The father knew what it all meant. He knew that the boy thought he would be very angry with him. He was grieved to think that his boy should have such feelings toward him. That is just exactly like the sinner. He thinks because he has sinned, God will have nothing to do with him. But what did that father do? Did he say, "Let the boy go"? No; he went after him. He arranged his business and started after the boy. He went from town to town, from city to city, He would get the ministers to let him preach, and at the close he would tell his story. "I have got a boy who is a wanderer on the face of the earth somewhere." He would describe his boy and say, "If you ever hear of him or see him, will you not write to me?" At last he found that he had gone to California. thousands of miles away. Did that father even then say, "Let him go"? No; off he went to the Pacific coast, seeking his boy. He went to San Francisco, and advertised in the news- papers that he would preach at such a church on such a day. When he had preached he told his story, in the hope that the boy might have seen the advertisement and come to the church. When he had done, away under the gallery there was a young man who waited until the audience had gone out; then he came towards the pulpit. The father looked, and saw it was his son, and he ran to him, and pressed him to his bosom. The boy wanted to confess what he had done, but not a word would the father hear. He forgave him freely, and took him to his home once more.

Oh, prodigal, you may be wandering on the dark mountains of sin, but God wants you to come home! The devil has been telling you lies about God; you think He will not receive you back. I tell you, He will welcome you this minute if you will come. Say, "I will arise and go to my Father." May God incline you to take this step! There is not one whom Jesus has not sought far longer than that father. There has not been a day since you left Him but He has followed you. I do not care what the past has been, or how black your life, He will receive you back. Arise then, O backslider, and come home once more to your Father's house.

Not long ago, in Edinburgh, a lady who was an earnest Christian worker, found a young woman whose feet had taken hold of hell, and who was pressing onward to a harlot's grave. The lady begged her to go back to her home, but she said no, her parents would never receive her. This Christian woman knew what a mother's heart was; so she sat down and wrote a letter to the girl's mother, telling her how she had met her daughter, who was sorry, and wanted to return. The next post brought an answer back, and on the envelope was written, "Immediate—immediate!" That showed a mother's heart. They opened the letter. Yes. she was forgiven. They wanted her back, and they sent money for her to come *immediately*.

Sinner, that is the proclamation, "Come *immediately*." That is what the great and loving God is saying to every wandering sinner—*immediately*. Yes, backslider, come home now. He will give you a warm welcome, and there will be joy in heaven over your return. Come now, for everything is ready.

III.

Now, let me speak to the third class, "If the righteous scarcely be saved, where shall the ungodly and the sinner appear?"

Sinner, what is to become of you? How shall you escape? *"Where art thou?"* Is it true that you are living without God and without hope in the world? Did you ever stop to think what would become of your soul if you should be taken away by a sudden stroke of illness—where you would stand in eternity? I read that the sinner is without God, without hope, and without excuse. If you are not saved, what excuse will you have to give? You cannot say that it is God's fault. He is only too anxious to save you. I want to tell you that you can be saved if you will. If you really want to pass from death to life, if you want to become an heir of eternal life, if you want to become a child of God, make up your mind that you will seek the kingdom of God now. I tell you upon the authority of His Word, that if you seek the kingdom of God you will find it. No man ever sought Christ with a sincere heart who did not find Him. I never knew a man make up his mind to have the question settled, but it was settled soon.

I am speaking to many who are in the prime of life, and I ask you, if you are not Christians, just to pause a few minutes and ask yourselves where you are. Let us look back on the hill that we have been climbing. What do we see? Yonder is the cradle. It is not far away. How short life is! It all seems but as yesterday.

Look along up the hill, and yonder is a tombstone; it marks the resting-place of a loved mother. When that mother died, did you not promise God that you would serve Him? Did you not say that your mother's God should become your God? And did you not take her hand in the stillness of the dying hour, and say, "Yes, mother, I will meet you in heaven"? And have you kept that promise? Are you trying to keep it? Ten years have rolled away, fifteen years—but are you any nearer God? Did the promise work any improvement in you? No, your heart is getting harder; the night is getting darker; by and by death will be throwing its shadows round you. My friend, where art thou?

Look again. A little further up the hill is another tombstone. It marks the resting-place of a little child. It may have been a lovely little girl; or it may have been a boy; and when that child was taken away from you, did you not promise God, and did you not promise the child, that you would meet it in heaven? Is the promise kept? Think! Are you still fighting against God? Are you still hardening your heart? Sermons that would have moved you five years ago—do they touch you now?

Once more look down the hill. Yonder there is a grave. You cannot tell how many days, or weeks, or years it is away. You are hastening towards that grave. Even should you live the life allotted to man, many are near the end; you are getting very feeble, and your locks are turning gray. It may be the coffin is already made that your body shall be laid in; it may be that the shroud is already waiting. My friend, is it not the height of madness to put off salvation so long? Why put off the question another day? Why say to the Lord Jesus once again, "Go Thy way for this time; when I have a convenient season, I will call for Thee"? Why not let Him come in now? Why not open your heart, and say, "King of glory, come in"?

Will there be a better opportunity? Did you not promise ten, fifteen, twenty, thirty years ago, that you would serve God? Perhaps you said you would do it when you got married and settled down; or when you were your own master. Have you attended to it?

You know there are

THREE STEPS TO THE LOST WORLD.

Let me give you their names.

The first is—*neglect*. All a man has to do is to neglect salvation, and that will take him to the lost world. Some people say, "What have I done?" Why, if you merely neglect salvation, you will be lost.

I am on a swift river, and lying in the bottom of my little boat. Down yonder, ten miles below, is the great cataract. Every one that goes over it perishes. I need not row the boat down. I have only to pull in the oars, and fold my arms, and *neglect*.

So all that a man has to do is to fold his arms in the current of life, and he will drift onward and be lost.

The second step is—*refusal*. If I met you and pressed this question on you, you would say, "Not now, Mr. Moody, not now." If I repeated, "I want you to press into the kingdom of God," you would politely refuse: "I will not become a Christian now, thank you. I know I ought, but I will not now."

Then the last step is to *despise* salvation. Some have already got on the lowest round of the ladder. You despise Christ, you hate Christ, you hate Christianity, you hate the best people on earth and the best friends you have got; and if I were to offer you the Bible, you would tear it up and put your foot upon it Oh, despisers! you will soon be in another world. Make haste and repent and turn to God.

Now, on which step are you, my friend; neglecting, or refusing, or despising? Bear in mind that a great many are taken off from the first step: they die in neglect. And a great many are taken away refusing. And a great many are on the last step, despising salvation. A few years ago they *neglected*, then tney began to *refuse,* and now they *despise* Christianity and Christ. They hate the sound of the church bell; they hate the Bible and the Christian; they curse the very ground we walk on. But one more step and they are gone. Oh, ye despisers, I set before you life and death; which will you choose? When Pilate had Christ on his hands, he said, "What shall I do with Him?" and the multitude cried out, "Away with Him! crucify Him!" Young men, is that your language now? Do you say, "Away with this gospel! Away with Christianity! Away with your prayers, your sermons, your gospel sounds! I do not want Christ"? Or will you be wise and say, "Lord Jesus, I want Thee, I need Thee, I will have Thee?"

Oh, may God bring you to this decision!

II.

"THERE IS NO DIFFERENCE."

ROMANS III. 22.

That is one of the hardest truths man has to learn. We are apt to think that we are just a little better than our neighbors, and if we find *they* are a little better than ourselves, we go to work and try to pull them down to our level. If you want to find out who and what man is, go to the third chapter of Romans, and there the whole story is told. "There is none righteous, no, not one." "All have sinned and come short." *All!* Some men like to have their lives written before they die. If you would like to read your biography, turn to this chapter, and you will find it already written.

I can imagine some one saying, "I wonder if he really pretends to say that 'there is no difference.'" The teetotaller asks, "Am I no better than the drunkard?" Well, I want to say right here that it is a good deal better to be temperate than intemperate; a good deal better to be honest than dishonest; it is better for a man even in this life to be upright in all his transactions than to cheat right and left. But when it comes to the great question of salvation, that does not touch the question at all, because "All have sinned and come short of the glory of God." Men are all bad by nature; the old Adam stock is bad, and we cannot bring forth good fruit until we are grafted into the one True Vine. If I have an orchard, and two apple trees in it, which both bear some bitter apples, perfectly worthless, does it make any difference to me that the one tree has got perhaps five hundred apples, all bad, and the other only two, both bad? There is no difference. One tree has more fruit than the other, but it is all *bad*. So it is with man. One thinks he has got only one or two very little sins— God won't notice them; while another man has broken every one of the ten commandments! No matter, there is no difference; they are both guilty; they have both broken the law. The law demands complete and perfect fulfilment, and if you cannot do that, you are lost, as far as the law is concerned. "Whosoever shall keep the whole law, and yet offend in one point, he is guilty of all."

Suppose you were to hang up a man to the roof with a chain of ten links; if one were to break, does it matter that the other nine are all sound and whole? Not the least. One link breaks, and down comes the man. But is it not rather hard that he should fall when the other nine are perfect and only one is broken? Why, of course not; if one is broken, it is just the same to the man as if all had been broken; he falls. So the man who breaks one commandment is guilty of all. He is a criminal in God's sight. Look at yonder prison, with its thousand victims. Some are there for murder, some for stealing, some for forgery, some for one thing and some for another. You may classify them, but every man is a *criminal*. They have all broken the law, and they are all paying the penalty. So the law has brought every man in a criminal in the sight of God.

If a man should advertise that he could take a correct photograph of people's hearts, do you believe he would find a customer? There is not a man among us whom you could hire to have his photograph taken, if you could photograph the real man. We go to have our faces taken, and carefully arrange our toilet, and if the artist flatters us, we say, "Oh, yes, that's a first-rate likeness," as we pass it round among our friends. But let the real man be brought out, the photograph of the heart, and see if a man will pass that round among his neighbors. Why, you would not want your own wife to see it! You would be frightened even to look at it yourself.

Nobody knows what is in that heart but Christ. We are told that "the heart is deceitful above all things, and desperately wicked; who can know it?" We do not know our own hearts; none of us have any idea how bad they are. Some bitter things are written against me, but I know a good many more things about myself that are bad than any other man. There is nothing good in the old Adam nature We have got a heart in rebellion against God by nature, and we do not even love God unless we are born of the Spirit. I can understand why men do not like this third chapter of Romans—it is too strong for them It speaks the truth too plainly. But just because we do not like it, we shall be all the better for having a look at it; very likely we shall find that it is exactly what we want, after all. It's a truth that men do not at all like, but I have noticed that the medicine that we do not like is the medicine that will do us good. If we do not think we are as bad as the description, we must just take a closer look at ourselves.

Here is a man who thinks he is not just so bad as it makes him out to be. He is sure he is a little better than his neighbor next door; he goes to church regularly and his neighbor never goes to church at all! "Of course," he congratulates himself, " I'll certainly get saved easier." But there is no use trying to evade it. God has given us the law to measure ourselves by, and by this most perfect rule we have all sinned and come short, and "there is no difference."

Paul brings in the law to show man that he is lost and ruined. God, being a perfect God, had to give a perfect law, and the law was given not to save men, but to measure them by. I want you to understand this clearly, because I believe hundreds and thousands stumble at this point. They try to save themselves by trying to keep the law; but it was never meant for men to save themselves by. The law has never saved a single man since the world began. Men have been trying to keep it, but they have never succeeded, and never will. Ask Paul what it was given for. Here is his answer, "That every mouth might be stopped, and the whole world become guilty before God." In this third chapter of Romans the world has been put on trial, and found guilty. The verdict has been brought in against us all —ministers and elders and church members, just as much as prodigals and drunkards—"ALL have sinned and come short."

The law stops every man's mouth. God will have a man humble himself down on his face before Him, with not a word to say for himself. Then God will speak to him, when he owns that he is a sinner, and gets rid of his own righteousness. I can always tell a man who has got near the kingdom of God; his mouth is stopped. If you will allow me the expression, God always shuts up a man's lips before He saves him. Job was not saved until he stopped talking about himself. Just see how God deals with him. First of all, He afflicts him, and Job begins to talk about his own goodness. "I delivered the poor," he says, "and the fatherless, and him who had none to help him. I was eyes to the blind, and feet was I to the lame. I was a father to the poor!" Why, they would have made Job an elder, if there had been elders in those days! He was a wonderfully good man! But now God says, "I'll put a few questions to you. Gird up now thy loins like a man; for I will demand of thee, and answer thou me." And Job is down directly; he is ashamed of himself; he cannot speak of his works any more. "Behold," he cries, "I am vile; what shall I answer Thee? I will lay mine hand upon my mouth." But he is not low enough yet, perhaps, and God puts a few more questions, "Ah" says Job, "I never understood these things before—I never saw it in that light." He is thoroughly humbled now; he can't help confessing it. "I have heard of Thee by hearing of the ear; but now mine eye seeth Thee. *Wherefore I abhor myself, and repent in dust and ashes.*" Now he has found his right position before God, and now God can talk to him. And God helps him, and raises him up, and gives him the double of all that he had before The clouds and the mist and the darkness around his path are driven away, and light from eternity bursts into his soul when he sees his nothingness in the sight of a pure and holy God.

This, then, is what God gives us the law for—to show us ourselves in our true colors.

I said to my family one morning a few weeks before the Chicago fire, "I am coming home this afternoon to give you a ride." My little boy clapped his hands. "Oh, papa, will you take me to see the bears in Lincoln

Park?" "Yes." You know boys are very fond of seeing bears. I had not been gone long when my little boy
said, "Mamma, I wish you would get me ready." "Oh,"
she said, "it will be a long time before papa comes."
"But I want to get ready, mamma." At last he was
ready to have the ride, face washed, and clothes all nice
and clean. "Now, you must take good care and not get
yourself dirty again," said mamma. Oh, of course he
was going to take care; he wasn't going to get dirty.
So off he ran to watch for me. However, it was a long
time yet until the afternoon, and after a little he began
to play. When I got home, I found him outside, with
his face all covered with dirt. "I can't take you to the
Park that way, Willie," "Why, papa? you said you
would take me." "Ah, but I can't; you're covered with
mud. I couldn't be seen with such a dirty little boy."
"Why I'se clean, papa; mamma washed me." "Well,
you've got dirty since." But he began to cry, and I
could not convince him that he was dirty. "I'se clean;
mamma washed me!" he cried. Do you think I argued
with him? No. I just took him up in my arms, and
carried him into the house, and showed him his face in
the looking-glass. He had not a word to say. He
would not take my word for it, but one look at the glass
was enough; he saw it for himself. He didn't say he
wasn't dirty after that!

Now the looking-glass showed him that his face was
dirty—*but I did not take the looking-glass to wash it;*
of course not. Yet that is just what thousands of people do.

THE LAW IS THE LOOKING-GLASS

to see ourselves in to show us how vile and worthless we
are in the sight of God; but people take the law, and try

to *wash* themselves with it! Man has been trying that for six thousand years, and has miserably failed. *By the deeds of the law there shall no flesh be justified in His sight.* Only one Man ever lived on the earth who could say He had kept the law, and that was the Lord Jesus Christ. If he had committed one sin, and come short in the smallest degree, His offering Himself for us would have been useless. But men have tried to do what He did, and have failed. Instead of sheltering under His righteousness, they have offered God their own. And God knew what a miserable failure it would be. "There is none righteous, no not one."

I don't care where you put man, everywhere he has been tried he has proved a total failure. He was put in Eden on trial. Some men say they wish they had Adam's chance. If they had, they would go down as quickly as he did. Put five hundred children into a hall, and give them ten thousand toys. Tell them they can run all over the hall, and they can have anything they want except one thing, placed, let us say, in one of the corners of Mr. Sankey's organ. Go out for a little, and do you not think that is the very first place they will go to? Why, nothing else in the room would have any attraction for them but just the thing they were told not to touch. And so let us not think Adam was any worse than ourselves. Adam was put on trial, and Satan walked into Eden. I do not know how long he was there, but I should think he had not been there twenty minutes before he stripped Adam of everything he had. There he is, fresh from the hands of his Creator; Satan comes upon the scene, and presents a temptation, and down he goes. *He was a failure.*

Then God took man into covenant with Him. He

said to Abraham, "Look yonder at the stars in the heav-ens and the sands on the seashore; I will make your seed like those. I will bless thee and multiply thee upon the earth." But what a stupendous failure man was under the covenant! Go back and read about it.

The Israelites are brought out of Egypt, see many signs and wonders, and stand at last at the foot of Mount Sinai. Then God's holy law is given to them. Did they not promise to keep it? "O yes," they cry, "we'll keep the law." To hear them talk you might think it was going to be all right now. But just wait till Joshua and Moses have turned their backs! No sooner have their leaders gone up the mountain to have an interview with God than they begin to say, "We wonder what has be. come of this man, Moses? we don't know where he has gone to. Come, let us make unto us another god. Aaron, make us a golden calf! Here are the golden orna-ments we got from the Egyptians. Come and make us another god!" When it is made, the people raise a great shout, and fall down and worship it. "Hark! lis-ten; what shout is that I hear?" says Moses, as he comes down the mountain side. "Alas," says Joshua, "there's war in the camp; it is the shout of the victor." "Ah no," says Moses, "it isn't the shout of victory or of war, Josh-ua; it is the cry of idolaters. They have forgotten the God who delivered them from the Egyptians, who led them through the Red Sea, who fed them with bread from heaven—angels' food. They have forgotten their promises to keep the commandments. Already the first two of them are broken, 'no other gods,' 'no graven image.' They've made them another god—a golden god!" And that's what men have been doing ever since.

Men worship the golden calf rather than the God of

heaven. Look around you. They bring before it health, and happiness, and peace. "Give me thirty pieces of silver, and I will sell you Christ," is the world's cry to-day. "Give me fashion, and I will sell you Christ!" "I will sacrifice my wife, my children, my life, my all, for a little drink. I will sell my soul for drink!" It is easy to blame those Israelites for worshiping the golden calf. But what are we doing ourselves? Ah, man was a *failure* then, and he has been a failure ever since.

Then God put him under the judges, and wonderful judges they were; but, once more, what a failure he was! After that came the prophets, and what a failure he was under them! Then came the Son Himself from heaven out of the bosom of the Father. He left the throne and came down here to teach us how to live. We took him and murdered Him on calvary! Man was a *failure* in Christ's time.

And now we are living under the dispensation of grace—a wonderful dispensation. God is showering down blessings from above. But what is man under grace? A stupendous failure. Look at that man reeling on his way to a drunkard's grave, and his soul going to a drunkard's hell! Look at the wretched harlots on your streets! Look at the profligacy and the pauperism and the loathsome sickness! Look at the vice and crime that festers everywhere, and tell me is it not true that man is a *failure* under grace?

Yes, man is a failure. I can see down the other side of the millennium. Christ has swayed His scepter over the earth for a thousand years; but man is a failure still, for "when the thousand years are expired, Satan shall be loosed out of his prison, and shall go out to deceive the nations which are in the four quarters of the earth. Gog and Magog, to gather them together to battle . . . and they compass the camp of the saints about, and the beloved city: and fire came down from God out of heaven, and devoured them." What man wants is another nature; he must be born again. What a foolish saying. "Experience teaches." Man has been a long time at that school, and has never learned his lesson yet— his own weakness and inability. He still thinks great things of his own strength. "I am going to stand after this," he says, "I have hit upon the right plan this time. I am able to keep the law now." But the first tempta- tion comes, and he is down. Man will not believe in God's strength. Man will not acknowledge himself a failure, and surrender to Christ to save him from his sins.

Is it not better to find out in this world that we are a failure, and to go to Christ for deliverance, than to sleep on and go down to hell without knowing we are sinners?

I know this doctrine that we have all failed, that we have all sinned and come short, is exceedingly objection- able to the natural man. If I had tried to find out the most disagreeable verse in the whole Bible, perhaps I could not have fastened upon one more universally dis- liked than "*There is no difference.*"

I can imagine Noah leaving his ark and going off preaching once in a while. As the passers-by stop to listen, there is no sound of the hammer or the plane. Noah has stopped work. He has gone off on a preaching tour, to warn his countrymen. Perhaps he tells them that a great deluge is coming to sweep away all the workers of iniquity; perhaps he warns them that *every* man who is not in the ark must perish; that there would be *no difference.* I can imagine one man saying, "You had better go back and finish your work, Noah, rather than come here preaching. You don't think we are going to believe in such nonsense as that! You tell us that all are going to perish alike! Do you really expect us to believe that the kings and governors, the sheriffs and the princes, the rulers, the beggars and thieves and harlots, are all going to be alike lost?" "Yes," says Noah; "the deluge that is coming by and by will take you all away—every man that is not in the ark must die. There will be no difference." Doubtless they thought Noah had gone raving mad. But did not the flood come and take them all away? Princes and paupers, and knaves and kings—was there any difference? No difference.

When the destroying angel was about to pass through Egypt, no doubt the haughty Egyptian laughed at the poor Israelite putting the blood on his door-post and lintel. "What a foolish notion," he would say, derisively; "the very idea of sprinkling blood on a door-post! If there *were* anything coming, that would never keep it away. I don't believe there is any death coming at all; and if it did, it might touch these poor people, but it would certainly never come near us." But when the night came, there was no difference. The king in his palace, the captive in his prison, the beggar by the wayside—they were all alike. Into every house the king of terrors had come, and there was universal mourning in the land. In the home of the poor and the lowly, in the home of the prince and the noble, in the home of governor and ruler, the eldest son lay dead. Only the poor Israelite escaped who had the blood on the door-post and lintel. And when God comes to us in judgment, if

we are not in Christ, all will be alike. Learned or un-
learned, high or low, priest or scribe—there will be no
difference.

Once more, I can imagine Abraham going down from
the hills to Sodom. He stands up, let us say, at the
corners of the streets, before Sodom was destroyed—"Ye
men of Sodom, I have a message from my God to you."
The people stand and look at the old man—you can see his
white locks as the wind sweeps through them. "I have
a warning for you," he cries; "God is going to destroy
the five cities of the plain, and every man who does not
escape to yonder mountain must perish. When He
comes to deal in judgment with you there will be no
difference; every man must die. The Lord Mayor, the
princes, the chief men, the mighty men, the judges, the
treasurers—all must perish. The thief and the vagabond,
and the drunkard—yes, all must perish alike. There
can be 'no difference.'" But these Sodomites answer,
"You had better go back to your tent on the hills,
Abraham. We don't believe a word of it. Sodom was
never so prosperous. Business was never so flourishing
as now. The sun never shone any brighter than it
does to-day. The lambs are skipping on the hills, and
everything moving on as it has done for centuries.
Don't preach that stuff to us; we don't believe it."
A few hours pass, and Sodom is in ashes! Did God
make any difference among those who would not believe?
No, God never utters any opinion; what He says is truth.
"All have sinned and come short," He cries; "and there
is no difference." I read of a deluge of fire that is
going to roll over this earth, and when God comes to
deal in judgment, there will be no difference, and every
man who is out of Christ must perish.

It was my sad lot to be in the Chicago fire. As the flames rolled down our streets, destroying everything in their onward march, I saw the great and the honorable, the learned and the wise, fleeing before the fire with the beggar and the thief and the harlot. All were alike. As the flames swept through the city it was like the judgment day. Neither the mayor, nor the mighty men, nor the wise men could stop those flames. They were all on a level then, and many who were worth hundreds of thousands were left paupers that night. When the day of judgment comes, there will be no difference. When the deluge came there was no difference; Noah's ark was worth more than all the world. The day before, it was the world's laughing-stock and if it had been put up to auction, you could not have got anybody to buy it except for firewood. But the deluge came, and then it was worth more than all the world together. And when the day of judgment comes, Christ will be worth more than all this world, more than ten thousand worlds. And if it was a terrible thing in the days of Noah to die outside the ark, it will be far more terrible for us to go down in our sins to a Christless grave.

Now I hope that you have seen what I have been trying to prove—that

WE ARE ALL SINNERS ALIKE.

I should like to use another illustration or two. I should like to make this truth so plain that a child might know it.

In the olden times in England, we are told, they used to have a game of firing arrows through a ring on the top of a pole. The man that failed to get all his arrows through the ring was called a "sinner." Now I should like for a moment to take up that illustration. Suppose our pole to be up in the gallery, and on the top of it the ring. I have got ten arrows, let us say, and Mr. Sankey has got another ten. I take up the first arrow, and take a good aim. Alas! I miss the mark. Therefore I am a "sinner." "But," I say, "I will do the best I can with the other nine. I have only missed with one." Like some men who try to keep all the commandments but one! I fire again, and miss the mark a second time. "Ah, but," I say, "I have got eight arrows still," and away goes another arrow—miss! I fire all the ten arrows and do not get one through the ring. Well, I was a "sinner" after the first miss, and I can only be a "sinner" after the tenth. Now Mr. Sankey comes with his ten arrows. He fires and gets his first arrow through. "Do you see that?" he says. "Well," I reply, "go on; don't boast until you get them all through." He takes the second arrow and gets that through. "Ha! do you see that?" "Don't boast," I repeat, "until all ten are through." If a man has not broken the law at all then he has got something to boast of! Away goes the third, and it goes through. Then another and another all right, and another until nine are through. "Now," he says, "one more arrow, and I am not a sinner." He takes up the last arrow, his hand trembles a little; he *just misses* the mark. *And he is a "sinner" as well as I am.*

My friend have you never missed the mark? Have you not come short? I should like to see the man who never missed the mark. *He never lived.*

Let me give you just one more illustration. When Chicago was a small town, it was incorporated and made a city. When we got our charter for the city, there was one clause in the constitution that allowed the Mayor to

appoint all the police. It worked very well when it was
a small city; but when it had three or four hundred
thousand inhabitants, it put too much power in the hands
of one man. So our leading citizens got a new bill
passed that took the power out of the hands of the Mayor,
and put it into the hands of Commissioners appointed
by government. There was one clause in the new law
that no man should be a policeman who was not a cer-
tain height—5 feet 6 inches, let us say. When the Commissioners got into power, they advertised for men as
candidates, and in the advertisement they stated that no
man need apply who could not bring good credentials to
recommend him. I remember going past the office one
day, and there was a crowd of men waiting to get in.
They quite blocked up the side of the street, and they
were comparing notes as to their chances of success
One said to another, " I have got a good letter of recom-
mendation from the Mayor, and one from the supreme
judge." Another said, "I have got a good letter from
Senator So-and-so. I'm sure to get in." The two men
come on together, and lay their letters down on the
Commissioners' desk. "Well," say the officials, "you
have certainly a good many letters, but we won't read
them till we measure you." Ah! they forgot all about
that. So the first man is measured, and he is only five
feet. "No chance for you, sir. The law says the man
must be 5 feet 6 inches, and you don't come up to the
standard." The other says, "Well, my chance is a good
deal better than his, I'm a good bit taller than he is"—
and he begins to measure himself by the other man.
That is what people are always doing, measuring themselves by others. Measure yourselves by the law of God,
or by the Son of God Himself; and if you do that, you

will find you have come short. He goes up to the offi-
cers, and they measure him; 5 feet 5 inches and nine-
tenths of an inch. "No good," they tell him; "you're not
up to the standard." "But I'm only one-tenth of an
inch short," he remonstrates. "It's no matter," they
say; "there's no difference." He goes with the man who
was five feet. One comes short six inches, and the
other only one-tenth of an inch, but the law cannot be
changed. And the law of God is that no man shall go
into the kingdom of heaven with *one* sin on him. He
that has broken the least law is guilty of all.

"Then, is there any hope for me?" you say. "What
star is there to relieve the midnight darkness and gloom?
What is to become of me? If all this is true, I am a
poor lost soul. I have committed sin from my earliest
childhood."

Thank God, my friends, this is just where the gospel
comes in. "He was made sin for us who knew no sin."
"He was wounded for our transgressions: He was bruised
for our iniquities; the chastisement of our peace was
upon Him, and with His stripes we are healed." "We
all like sheep have gone astray, we have turned every
one to his own way, and the Lord *hath laid* on Him
the iniquity of us all."

You ask me what my hope is; it is that Christ died
for my sins, in my stead, in my place, and therefore I
can enter into life eternal. You ask Paul what his hope
was. "Christ died for our sins according to the Scripture." This is the hope in which died all the glorious
martyrs of old, in which all who have entered heaven's
gate have found their only comfort. Take that doctrine
of substitution out of the Bible, and my hope is lost
With the law, without Christ, we are all undone. The

law we have broken, and it can only hang over our head the sharp sword of justice. Even if we could keep it from this moment, there remains the unforgiven past. "Without shedding of blood there is no remission."

There is a well-known story told of Napoleon the First's time. In one of the conscriptions, during one of his many wars, a man was balloted as a conscript who did not want to go, but he had a friend who offered to go in his place. His friend joined the regiment in his name, and was sent off to the war. By and by a battle came on, in which he was killed, and they buried him on the battle-field. Some time after the Emperor wanted more men, and by some mistake the first man was balloted a second time. They went to take him, but he remonstrated. "You cannot take me." "Why not?" "I am dead," was the reply. "You are not dead; you are alive and well." "But I *am* dead," he said. "Why, man, you must be mad! Where did you die?" "At such a battle, and you left me buried on such a battle-field." "You talk like a madman," they cried; but the man stuck to his point that he had been dead and buried some months. "Look up your books," he said, "and see if it is not so." They looked, and found that he was right. They found the man's name entered as drafted, sent to the war, and marked off as killed. "Look here," they said, "you didn't die. You must have got some one to go for you. It must have been your *substitute*." "I know that," he said; "he died in my stead. You cannot touch me. I died in that man, and now I go free. The law has no claim against me." They would not recognize the doctrine of substitution, and the case was carried to the emperor, who said that the man was right, that he was dead and buried in the eyes of the law, and that France had no claim against him.

The story may be true, or may not, but one thing I know to be true, that the Emperor of heaven recognizes the doctrine of substitution. Christ died for me; that is my hope of eternal life. "There is no condemnation to them which are in Christ Jesus." If you ask me what you must do to share this blessing, I answer—go and deal personally with Christ about it. Take the sinner's place at the foot of the cross. Strip yourself of all your own righteousness, and put on Christ's. Wrap yourself up in His perfect robe, and receive Him by simple trust as your own Savior. Thus you inherit the priceless treasures that Christ hath purchased with His blood. "*As many as received Him, to them gave He power to become the sons of God.*" Yes, sons of God: power to overcome the world, the flesh, and the devil; power to crucify every besetting sin, passion, lust; power to shout in triumph over every trouble and temptation of your life, "I can do all things through Christ which strengtheneth me."

I have been trying to tell you the old, old tale that men are sinners. I may be speaking to some one, perhaps, who thinks it a waste of time. "God knows I'm a sinner," he cries; "you don't need to prove it. Since I could speak, I've done nothing but break every law of earth and heaven." Well, my friend, I have good news for you. It is just as easy for God to save you who have broken the whole decalogue, as the man who has only broken one of the commandments. Both are dead— dead in sins. It is no matter how *dead* you are, or how long you have been dead; Christ can bring you to life just the same. There is no difference. When Christ met that poor widow coming out of Nain, following the body of her darling boy to the grave—he was just newly dead—His loving heart could not pass her; He stopped the funeral, and bade the dead arise. He was obeyed at once, and the mother was clasped once more in the living embrace of her son. And when Jesus stood by the grave of Lazarus, who had been dead *four* days, was it not just as easy for Him to say, "Lazarus, come forth"? Was it not as easy for Him to bring Lazarus from his tomb, who had been dead four days, as the son of the widow, who had been dead but one? Yes, it was just as easy; there was no difference. They were both alike dead, and Christ raised the one just as easily, and as willingly, and as lovingly as the other. And therefore, my friend, you need not complain that Christ cannot save you. Christ died *for the ungodly,* and if you turn to Him at this moment with an honest heart, and receive Him simply as your Savior and your God I have the authority of His Word for telling you that He will *in no wise cast you out.*

And you who have never felt the burden of your sin —you who think there is a great deal of difference—you who thank God that you are not as other men—beware! God has nothing to say to the self-righteous. Unless you humble yourself before Him in the dust, and confess before Him your iniquities and sins, the gate of heaven, which is open only for *sinners saved by grace,* must be shut against you forever!

III.

GOOD NEWS.

"THE GOSPEL."—1 COR. XV. I.

I hardly think there is a word in the English language so little understood as the word "gospel." We hear it every day, and we have heard it from our earliest childhood, yet there are many people; and even many Christians, who do not really know what it means. I believe I was a child of God a long time before I really knew.

The word "gospel" means "God's spell," or good spell, or, in other words, "good news."

The gospel is *good tidings of great joy.* No better news ever came out of heaven than the gospel. No better news ever fell upon the ears of the family of man than the gospel. When the angels came down to proclaim the tidings, what did they say to those shepherds on the plains of Bethlehem? "Behold, I bring you *sad* tidings"? No! "Behold, I bring you *bad* news"? No! "Behold, I bring you *good* tidings of *great joy*, which shall be to all people; for unto you is born this day, in the city of David, a Savior."

If those shepherds had been like a good many people at the present time, they would have said, "We do not believe it is good news. It is all excitement. These angels want to get up a revival. These angels are trying to excite us. Don't believe them." That is what Satan is saying now. "Don't believe that the gospel is good news; it will only make you miserable." He knows that the moment a man *believes* good news, he just *receives* it. And so no one who is under the power of the devil really believes that the gospel is good news. But those shepherds believed the message that the angels brought, and their hearts were filled with joy.

If a boy came with a despatch to some one, could you not tell by the receiver's looks what kind of a message it was? If it brought good news, you would see it in his face in a moment. If it told him that his boy, away in some foreign land, a prodigal son, had come to himself, like the one in the 15th of Luke, do you not think the father's face would light up with joy? And he would pass the good news on to his wife, and her face would brighten too, as she shared his joy. But the tidings that the gospel brings are more glorious than that. We are dead in trespasses and sins, and the gospel offers life. We are enemies to God, and the gospel offers reconciliation. The world is in darkness, and the gospel offers light. Because man will not believe the gospel, that Christ is the light of the world, the world is dark to-day. But the moment a man believes, the light from Calvary streams upon his path, and he walks in an unclouded sun.

I want to tell you why I like the gospel. It is because it has been

THE VERY BEST NEWS I HAVE EVER HEARD.

That is just why I like to preach it, because it has done me so much good. No man can ever tell what it has done for him, but I think I can tell what it has *undone*. It has taken out of my path three of the bitterest enemies I ever had.

There is that terrible enemy mentioned in 1 Cor. **xv.**, the last enemy,

DEATH.

The gospel has taken it out of the way. My mind very often runs back many years, before I was converted, and I think how dark it used to seem as I thought of the future. I well remember how I used to look on death as a terrible monster, how he used to throw his dark shadow across my path; how I trembled as I thought of the terrible hour when he should come for me; how I thought I should like to die of some lingering disease, such as consumption, so that I might know when he was coming. It was the custom in our village to toll from the old church bell the age of any one who died. Death never entered that village and tore away one of the inhabitants but I counted the tolling of the bell. Sometimes it was seventy, sometimes eighty; sometimes it would be down among the teens, sometimes it would toll out the death of some one of my own age. It made a solemn impression upon me. I felt a coward then. I thought of the cold hand of death feeling for the cords of life. I thought of being launched forth to spend my eternity in an unknown land.

As I looked into the grave, and saw the sexton throw the earth on the coffin-lid, "Earth to earth—ashes to ashes—dust to dust," it seemed like the death-knell to my soul.

But that is all changed now. The grave has lost its terror. As I go on towards heaven I can shout—"O death! where is thy sting?" and I hear the answer rolling down from Calvary—"buried in the bosom of the Son of God." He took the sting right out of death for me and received it into His own bosom. Take a hornet and pluck the sting out; you are not afraid of it after that any more than of a fly. So death has lost its sting. That last enemy has been overcome, and I can look on death as a crushed victim. All that death can get now is this old Adam, and I do not care how quickly I get rid of it. I shall get a glorified body, a resurrection body, a body much better than this.

Suppose death should come stealing up into this pulpit, and lay his icy hand upon my heart, and it should cease to throb, I should rise to the better world to be present with the King. The gospel has made an enemy a friend. What a glorious thought, that when you die you only sink into the arms of Jesus, to be borne to the land of everlasting rest! "To die," the apostle says, "is gain."

I can imagine when they laid our Lord in Joseph's tomb one might have seen death sitting over that sepulcher, saying, "I have Him; He is my victim. He said He was the Resurrection and the Life. Now I hold Him in my cold embrace. They thought He was never going to die; but see Him now. He has had to pay tribute to me." Never! The glorious morning comes, the Son of man bursts asunder the bands of death, and rises, a Conqueror, from the grave. "Because I live," He shouts, "ye shall live also." Yes, *ye shall live also*—is it not good news? Ah, my friends, there is no bad news about a gospel which makes it so sweet to live, so sweet to die.

Another terrible enemy that troubled me was

SIN.

What a terrible hour I thought it would be, when my sins from childhood, every secret thought, every evil desire, everything done in the dark, should be brought to light, and spread out before an assembled universe! Thank God, these thoughts are gone. The gospel tells me my sins are all put away in Christ. Out of love to me God has taken all my sins and cast them behind His back. That is a safe place for them. God never turns back; He always marches on. He will never see your sins if they are behind His back—that is one of His own illustrations. Satan has to get behind God to find them. How far away are they, and can they ever come back again? "*As far as the east is from the west, so far hath He removed our transgressions from us.*"

Not *some* of them; He takes them *all* away. You may pile up your sins till they rise like a dark mountain, and then multiply them by ten thousand for those you cannot think of; and after you have tried to enumerate all the sins you have ever committed, just let me bring one verse in, and that mountain will melt away: "The blood of Jesus Christ, His Son, cleanseth us from ALL sin." In Ireland, some time ago, a teacher asked a little boy if there was anything God could not do, and the little fellow said, "Yes; He can not see my sins through the blood of Christ." That is just what He cannot do. The blood covers them. Is it not good news that you can get rid of sin? You come to Christ a sinner, and if you receive His gospel your sins are taken away. You are invited to do this; nay, He entreats you to do it. You are invited to make an exchange; to get rid of all your sins, and to take Christ and His righteousness in the place of them.

Is not that good news?

There is another enemy which used to trouble me a great deal—

JUDGMENT.

I use to look forward to the terrible day when I should be summoned before God. I could not tell whether I should hear the voice of Christ saying, "Depart from me, ye cursed," or whether it would be, "Enter thou into the joy of thy Lord"; and I thought that till he stood before the great white throne, no man could tell whether he was to be on the right hand or the left. But the gospel tells me that is already settled: "There is now *no condemnation* to them that are in Christ Jesus." "Verily, verily"—and when you see that word in Scripture, you may know there is something very important coming—"Verily, verily, I say unto you, he that heareth my word, and believeth on Him that sent me, *hath* everlasting life, and *shall not come into condemnation*, but *is passed* from death unto life." Well, now, I am not coming into judgment for sin. It is no open question. God's Word has settled it. Christ was judged for me, and died in my stead, and I go free. He that believeth "*hath*"—h-a-t-h, hath. Is not that good news?

A man prayed for me once that I might obtain eternal life *at last*. I could not have said Amen to that. If he meant it in this sense, I obtained eternal life many years ago, when I was converted. What is the gift of God, if it is not eternal life? And what makes the gospel such good news? Is it not that it offers eternal life to every poor sinner who will take it?

If an angel came straight from the throne of God, and proclaimed that God had sent him here to offer us any one thing we might ask—that each one should have his own petition granted—what would be your cry? There would be but one response, and the cry would

make heaven ring: "Eternal life! eternal life!" Everything else would float away into nothingness. It is
life men want, men value most. Let a man worth a
million dollars be on a wrecked vessel, and if he could
save his life for six months by giving that million, he
would give it in an instant. But the gospel is not a
six months' gift. "*The gift of God is eternal life.*"
And is it not one of the greatest marvels that men have
to stand and plead and pray and beseech their fellow-
men to take this precious gift of God?

My friend, there is one spot on earth where the fear of
Death, of Sin, and of Judgment, need never trouble us,
the only safe spot on earth where the sinner can stand—
Calvary. Out on the western prairies, in the autumn,
when men go hunting, and there has not been any rain
for months, sometimes the prairie grass catches fire.
Sometimes, when the wind is strong, the flames may be
seen rolling along, twenty feet high, destroying man
and beast in their onward rush. When the frontiers-
men see what is coming, what do they do to escape?
They know they cannot run as fast as that fire can run.
Not the fleetest horse can escape it. They just take a
match and light the grass around them. The flames
sweep onwards; they take their stand in the burnt dis-
trict, and are safe. They hear the flames roar as they
come along. They see death bearing down upon them
with resistless fury, but they do not fear. They do not
even tremble as the ocean of flame surges around them,
for over the place where they stand the fire has already
passed, and there is no danger. There is nothing for
the fire to burn. And there is one spot on earth that
God has swept over. Eighteen hundred years ago
the storm burst on Calvary, and the Son of God took

it into His own bosom, and now, if we take our stand by the cross, we are safe for time and for eternity.

Sinner, would you be safe now? Would you be free from the condemnation of the sins that are past, from the power of the temptations that are to come? Then take your stand on the Rock of Ages. Let death, let the grave, let the judgment come, the victory is Christ's, and yours through Him. Oh, will you not receive this gospel now—this wonderful message of His sacrifice for you?

Some people when the gospel is preached, put on a long face, as if they had to attend a funeral or witness an execution, or hear some dry, stupid lecture or sermon. It was my privilege to go into Richmond with General Grant's army. I had not been long there before it was announced that the negroes were going to have a jubilee meeting. These colored people were just coming into liberty; their chains were falling off, and they were just awakening to the fact that they were free. I thought it would be a great event, and I went down to the African Church, one of the largest in the South, and found it crowded. One of the colored chaplains of a northern regiment had offered to speak. I have heard many eloquent men in E rope and America, but I do not think I ever heard eloquence such as I heard that day.

He said, "Mothers! rejoice to-day; you are forever free! That little child has been torn from your embrace and sold off to some distant state for the last time. Your hearts are never to be broken again in that way; you are free!" The women clapped their hands and shouted at the top of their voices, "Glory, glory to God!" It was good news to them, and they believed it. It filled them full of joy.

Then the preacher turned to the young men, and said, "Young men! rejoice to-day! You have heard the crack of the slave-driver's whip for the last time. Your posterity shall be free. Young men, rejoice to-day, you are forever free!" And they clapped their hands and shouted, "Glory to God!" They believed the good tidings.

"Young maidens!" the speaker continued, "rejoice to-day! You have been put on the auction-block and sold for the last time. You are free—forever free!" They believed it, and lifting up their voices, shouted, "Glory be to God!" I never was in such a meeting. They *believed* that it was good news to them.

My friend, I bring you better tidings than that. No colored man or woman ever had such a mean, wicked, cruel master as those that are serving Satan. Do I speak to a man who is a slave to strong drink? Christ can give you strength to hurl the cup from you, and make you a sober man, a loving husband, a kind father. Yes, poor wife of the drunkard, I bring you good news; your husband may become a sober man again. And you, poor sinner, you who have been so rebellious and and wayward, the gospel brings a message of forgiveness to you. God wants you to be reconciled to Him. "Be ye reconciled to God." It is His message to you—

A MESSAGE OF FRIENDSHIP.

Here is a little story of reconciliation; perhaps it may help you:—

An Englishman had an only son; and only sons are often petted, and humored, and ruined. This boy became very headstrong, and often he and his father had trouble. One day they had a quarrel, and the father was very angry, and so was the son; and the father said he wished the boy would leave home and never come back. The boy said he would go, and would not come into his father's house again till he sent for him. The father said he would never send for him. Well, away went the boy. But when a father gives up a boy, a mother does not.

You know there is no love on earth so strong as a mother's love. A great many things may separate a man and his wife; a great many things may separate a father from a son; but there is nothing in the wide world that can ever separate a true mother from her child. To be sure there are some mothers that have drunk so much liquor that they have drunk up all their affection. But I am talking about a true mother; and she will never cast off her boy.

The mother began to write and plead with the boy to write to his father first, and he would forgive him; but the boy said, "I will never go home till father asks me." Then she pled with the father, but the father said, "No, I will never ask him." At last she came down to her sick=bed, broken=hearted, and when she was given up by the physicians to die, the husband, anxious to gratify her last wish, wanted to know if there was anything he could do for her before she died. She gave him a look; he well knew what it meant. Then she said, "Yes, there is one thing you can do. You can send for my boy. That is the only wish on earth you can gratify. If you do not pity him and love him when I am dead and gone, who will"? "Well," said the father, "I will send word to him that you want to see him." "No," she says, "you know he will not come for me. If ever I see him you must send for him." At last the father went to his office and wrote a despatch in his own name, asking the boy to come home. As soon as he got the invitation from his father he started off to see his dying mother. When he opened the door to go in he found his mother dying, and his father by the bedside. The father heard the door open, and saw the boy, but instead of going to meet him he went to another part of the room, and refused to speak to him. His mother seized his hand—how she had longed to press it! She kissed him, and then said, "Now, my son, just speak to your father. You speak first, and it will all be over." But the boy said, "No, mother, I will not speak to him until he speaks to me." She took her husband's hand in one hand, and the boy's in the other, and spent her dying moments in trying to bring about a reconciliation. Then just as she was expiring—she could not speak— so she put the hand of the wayward boy into the hand of the father and passed away! The boy looked at his mother, the father at his wife, and at last the father's heart broke, and he opened his arms, and took that boy to his bosom, and beside that dead body they were reconciled.

Sinner, this is only a faint type, a poor illustration, because God is not angry with you. I bring you to the dead body of Christ. I ask you to look at the wounds in His hands and feet, and the wound in His side, and I ask you, "Will you not be reconciled?" When Christ left heaven, He went down into the manger that He might get hold of the vilest sinner, and put the hand of the wayward prodigal into that of the Father, and He died that you and I might be reconciled. If you take my advice you will not sleep to-night until you are reconciled. "Be ye reconciled."

Oh, this gospel of reconciliation! My friend, is it not a glad gospel?

And then it is

A FREE GOSPEL.

Any one may have it. You need not ask, "For whom is this good news?" It is for yourself. If you would like Christ's own word for it, come with me to that scene in Jerusalem where the disciples are bidding Him farewell. Calvary with all of its horrors is behind Him, Gethsemane is over, and Pilate's judgment hall. He He has passed the grave, and is about to take His place at the right hand of the Father. Around Him stands His little band of disciples, the little church He was to leave behind Him to be His witnesses. The hour of parting has come, and He has some "last words" for them. Is He thinking about Himself in these closing moments? Is He thinking about the throne that is waiting Him, and the Father's smile that will welcome Him to heaven? Is He going over in memory the scenes of the past, or is He thinking of the friends who have followed Him so far, who will miss Him so much when He is gone? No, He is thinking about *you*. You imagined He would think of those who loved Him? No, sinner, He thought of you then. He thought of His enemies, those who shunned Him, those who despised Him, those who killed him—He thought what more He could do for them. He thought of those who would hate Him, of those who would have none of His gospel, of those who would say it was too good to be true, of those who would make the excuse that He never died for *them*. And then turning to His disciples, His heart bursting with compassion, He gave them His farewell charge,

Go ye into ALL the world and preach the gospel TO

EVERY CREATURE." They are almost His last words, "to every creature."

I can imagine Peter saying, "Lord, do you really mean that we shall preach the gospel to *every* creature?" "Yes, Peter." "Shall we go back to Jerusalem and preach the gospel to those Jerusalem sinners who murdered you?"

"Yes, Peter, go back and tarry there until you are endued with power from on high. Offer the gospel to them first. Go search out that man who spat in my face. Tell him I forgive him. There is nothing in my heart but love for him. Go, search out the man who put that cruel crown of thorns on my brow. Tell him I will have a crown ready for him in my kingdom, if he will accept salvation. There shall not be a thorn in it, and he shall wear it forever and ever in the kingdom of his Redeemer. Find out that man who took the reed from my hand, and smote my head, driving the thorns deeper into my brow. If he will accept salvation as a gift, I will give him a scepter, and he shall sway it over the nations of the earth. Yes, I will give him to sit with me upon my throne. Go, seek that man who struck me with the palm of his hand. Find him, and preach the gospel to him. Tell him that the blood of Jesus Christ cleanseth from all sin, and my blood was shed for him freely." Yes, I can imagine Him saying, "Go, seek out that poor soldier who drove the spear into my side. Tell him that there is a nearer way to my heart than that. Tell him that I forgive him freely, and that I will make him a soldier of the cross, and my banner over him shall be love."

I thank God that the gospel is to be preached to *every* creature. I thank God the commission is so free. There is no man so far gone but the grace of God can reach him; no man so desperate or so black, but He will

forgive him.   Yes, I thank God I can preach the gospel
to the man or woman who is is as black as hell itself.
I thank God for the "whosoevers" of the invitations of
Christ.   "God so loved the world that He gave His
only-begotten Son, that *whosoever* believeth on Him
should not perish, but have everlasting life," and
" *Whosoever will* let him take the water of life freely."

I heard of a woman once who thought there was
no promise in the Bible for her; they were all for other
people.   One day she got a letter, and when she opened
it, found it was not for her at all, but for some other
woman of the same name.   It led her to ask herself,
"If I should find some promise in the Bible directed to
me, how should I know it meant *me*, and not some other
woman?"   And she found out that she must just take
God at His Word, and include herself among the "whosoevers" and the "every creatures" to whom the gospel
is freely preached.

I know that the word "whosoever" means every man,
every woman, every child in this wide world.   It means
the boy, the grey-haired man, the maiden in the blush
of youth, the young man breaking a mother's heart, the
drunkard steeped in misery and sin.   O my friend, will
you not believe this good news?   Will you not receive
this wonderful gospel of Christ?   Will you not believe,
poor sinner, that it means *you*?   Will you say it is too
good to be true?

I was in Ohio a few years ago, and was invited to
preach in the State prison.   Eleven hundred convicts
were brought into the chapel, and all sat in front of me.
After I had finished preaching, the chaplain said to
me: "Mr. Moody, I want to tell you of a scene which
occurred in this room.   A few years ago, our com-

missioners went to the governor of the State, and got him to promise that he would pardon five men for good behavior. The governor consented, with this under-standing—that the record was to be kept secret, and that at the end of six months, the men highest on the roll should receive a pardon, regardless of who or what they were. At the end of six months the prisoners were all brought into the chapel. The commissioners came, and the President stood on the platform, and putting his hand in his pocket, brought out some papers, and said, 'I hold in my hand pardons for five men.'"

The chaplain told me he never witnessed anything on earth like it. Every man was as still as death. Many were deadly pale. The suspense was awful. It seemed as if every heart had ceased to beat.

The commissioner went on to tell them how they had got the pardon; but the chaplain interrupted him. "Before you make your speech, read out the names. This suspense is awful." So he read out out the first name, "Reuben Johnson will come and get his pardon"; and he held it out, but no one came forward. He said to the governor, "Are all the prisoners here?" The governor told him they were all there. Then he said again, "Reuben Johnson will come and get his pardon. It is signed and sealed by the governor. He is a free man." Not one moved. The chaplain told me he looked right down where Reuben was. He was well known. He had been nineteen years there, and many were looking around to see him spring to his feet. But he himself was looking round to see the fortunate man who had got his pardon. Finally the chaplain caught his eye, and said, "Reuben, you are the man." Reuben turned around and looked behind him to see where Reuben was. The chaplain said the second time, "Reuben, *you* are the man"; and a second time he looked round, thinking it must be some other Reuben.

So men do not believe the gospel is for them. They think it is too good, and pass it over their shoulders to the next man. But *you* are the man now.

Well, the chaplain could see where Reuben was, and he had to say three times, "Reuben, come and get your pardon." At last the truth began to steal over the the old man. He got up and came along down the hall, trembling from head to foot, and when he got the pardon he looked at it and went back to his seat and buried his face in his hands, and wept. When the prisoners got into the ranks to go back to the cells, Reuben got into the ranks too, and the chaplain had to call to him, "Reuben, get out of the ranks; you are a free man, you are no longer a prisoner." And Reuben stepped out of the ranks. He was free!

That is the way men make out pardons. They make them out for good character or good behavior. But God makes out pardons for men who have not got any character, who have been very, very bad. He offers a pardon to every sinner on earth if he will take it. I do not care who he is or what he is like. He may be the greatest libertine that ever walked the streets, or the greatest blackguard who ever lived, or the greatest drunkard, or thief, or vagabond; but I come with glad tidings, and preach the gospel to *every creature*.

IV.

CHRIST SEEKING SINNERS.

"THE SON OF MAN CAME TO SEEK AND TO SAVE
THAT WHICH WAS LOST."—LUKE XIX. 10.

To me this is one of the sweetest verses in the whole
Bible. In this one little short sentence we are told
what Christ came into this world for. He came for a
purpose, He came to do a work; and in this little verse
the whole story is told. He came not to condemn the
world, but that the world through Him might be
saved.

A few years ago the Prince of Wales came to America,
and there was great excitement. The papers took it up,
and began to discuss it, and a great many were wonder-
ing what he came for. Was it to look into the republi-
can form of government? Was it for his health? Was it
to see our institutions? or for this, or for that? He came
and went, but he never told us what he came for. But
when the Prince of heaven came down into this world,
He told us what He came for. God sent Him, and He
came to do the will of His Father. What was that?
"To seek and to save that which was lost."

You cannot find any place in Scripture where a man
was sent by God to do a work in which he failed. God
sent Moses to Egypt to bring three millions of bond-
men out of the house of bondage into the Promised
Land. Did he fail? It looked, at first, as if he were
going to. If we had been in the Court when Pharaoh

said to Moses, "Who is God, that I should obey Him?" and ordered him out of his presence, we might have thought it meant failure. But did it? God sent Elijah to stand before Ahab, and it was a bold thing when he told him there should be neither dew nor rain; but didn't he lock up the heavens for three years and six months? Now here is God sending His own beloved Son from His bosom, from the throne, down into this world. Do you think He is going to fail? Thanks be to God, He can save to the uttermost, and there is not a man in the world who may not find it so, if he is willing to be saved.

I find a great blessing to myself in taking up a passage like this, and looking all round it, to see what brought it out. If you look back to the close of the eighteenth chapter, you will find Christ coming near the city of Jericho. Sitting by the wayside was a poor, blind beggar. Perhaps he had been there for years, led out, it may be, by one of his children, or perhaps, as we sometimes see, he had a dog to lead him out. There he had sat for years, and his cry had been, "Please give a poor blind man some money." One day, as he was sitting there, a man came down from Jerusalem, and seeing him, took his seat by his side, and said, "Bartimeus, I have good news for you." "What is it?" said the blind beggar. "There is a man in Israel who is able to give you sight." "Oh no," said the blind beggar, "there is no chance of my ever receiving sight. I was born blind, and nobody born blind ever got sight. I shall never see in this world. I may in the world to come, but I must go through this world blind." "But," said the man, "let me tell you. I was at Jerusalem the other day, and the great Galilean prophet was there, and I saw a man who was born blind that had received his sight; and I never saw a man with better sight. He does not need to use glasses. He can see quite clearly." Then for the first time, hope rose in the poor man's heart, and he asked, "How was it done?" "Why, Jesus spat on the ground and made some clay, and anointed his eyes," (that is enough to put a man's sight out, even if he can see!) "and sent him to wash in the pool of Siloam; and while he was doing so he got two good eyes. Yes, it is so. I talked with him, and I didn't see a man in all Jerusalem who had better sight." "What did he charge?" said Bartimeus. "Nothing. There was no fee or doctor's bill. He got his sight for nothing. You just tell Him what you want; you don't need to have an influential committee to call on Him, or any important deputation. The poor have as much influence with Him as the rich; all are alike." "What is His name?" asked Bartimeus. "Jesus of Nazareth; and if He ever comes this way, don't let Him by without getting your case laid before Him." And the blind man said, "That you may be sure of. He shall never pass this way without my seeking Him."

A day or two after, he was led out, and took his seat at the usual place, still crying out for money, All at once, he heard the footsteps of a coming multitude, and asked, "Who is it? Tell me, who is it?" Some one said it was Jesus of Nazareth that was passing by. The moment he heard that, he said to himself, "Why, that is the man who gives sight to the blind," and he lifted up his cry, "Jesus, thou son of David, have mercy upon me!" I don't know who it was —perhaps it was Peter —who said to him, "Hush! keep still." He thought the Lord was going up to Jerusalem to be crowned king, and he would not like to be disturbed by a poor blind beggar.

Oh, they did not know the Son of God when He was here! He would hush every harp in heaven to hear a sinner pray; no music delights Him so much.

But Bartimeus lifted up his voice louder, "Thou Son of David, have mercy on me." His prayer reached the ear of the Son of God, as prayer always will, and His footsteps were arrested. He told them to bring the man. "Bartimeus," they said, "be of good cheer. Arise, He calleth thee"; and He never called any one, but He had something good in store for him. Oh, sinner! remember that. They led the blind man to Jesus. The Lord said, "What shall I do for you?" "Lord, that I may receive my sight." "You shall have it," the Lord said; and straightway his eyes were opened.

I should have liked to have been there, to see that wonderful scene. The first object that met his gaze was the Son of God Himself, and now among the shouting multitude, no one shouts louder than the poor blind man that has got his sight. He glorifies God, and I fancy I can hear him shouting, "Hosanna to the Son of David."

Pardon me, if I now draw a little on my imagination. Bartimeus gets into Jericho, and he says, "I will go and see my wife, and tell her about it." A young convert always wants to talk to his friends about salvation. Away he goes down the street, and he meets a man who passes him, goes on a few yards, and then turns round and says, "Bartimeus, is that you?" "Yes." "Well, I thought it was, but I could not believe my eyes. How have you got your sight?" "Oh, I just met Jesus of Nazareth outside the city, and asked Him to have mercy on me." "Jesus of Nazareth! What, is He in this part of

the country?" "Yes. He is right here in Jericho.
He is now going down to the western gate." "I should
like to see Him," says the man, and away he runs down
the street; but he cannot catch a glimpse of Him, even
though he stands on tip-toe, being little of stature, and
on account of the great throng around Him. "Well,"
he says, "I am not going to be disappointed "; so he runs
on, and climbs up into a sycamore tree. "If I can get
on to that branch, hanging right over the highway, He
cannot pass without my getting a good look at Him."

That must have been a very strange sight to see the
rich man climbing up a tree like a boy, and hiding
among the leaves, where he thought nobody would see
him, to get a glimpse of the passing stranger!

There comes the crowd bursting out, and he looks for
Jesus. He looks at Peter; "That's not He." He looks
at John; "That's not He." At last his eye rests on One
fairer than the sons of men; "That's He!" And Zaccheus, just peeping out from among the branches, looks
down upon the wonderful God-man in amazement. At
last the crowd comes to the tree. It looks as if Christ
is going by, but He stops right under the tree, looks up,
and says, "Zaccheus, make haste and come down."

I can imagine, the first thought in his mind was,
"Who told Him my name? I was never introduced to
Him." Ah! He knew him. Sinner, Christ knows all
about you. He knows your name and your house. You
need not try to hide from Him. He knows where you
are, and all about you.

Some people do not believe in

SUDDEN CONVERSION.

I should like them to answer me—when was Zaccheus

converted? He was certainly in his sins when he went up into the tree; he certainly was converted when he came down. He must have been converted somewhere between the branch and the ground. It didn't take a long while to convert that publican! " Make haste and come down. I shall never pass this way again. This is my last visit." Zaccheus made haste and came down, and received Him joyfully. Did you ever hear of any one receiving Christ in any other way? He received Him joyfully. Christ brings joy with Him. Sin, gloom, and darkness flee away; light, peace and joy burst into the soul. Reader, may you come down from your high place, and receive Christ now.

Some one may ask, "How do you know that he was converted?" I think he gave very good evidence. I would like to see as fruitful evidence of conversion now-a-days. Let some rich men be converted, and give half their goods to feed the poor, and people will believe pretty quickly that it is genuine work! But there is better evidence even than that. "If I have taken anything from any man falsely, *I restore him fourfold.*" Very good evidence that. You say if people are converted suddenly, they won't hold out. Zaccheus held out long enough to restore fourfold. We should like to have a work that reaches men's pockets.

I can imagine one of his servants going to a neighbor next morning, with a check for $100, and handing it over. "What is this for?" "Oh, my master defrauded you out of $25 a few years ago, and this is restitution money." That would give confidence in Zaccheus' conversion! I wish a few cases like that would happen now, and then people would stop talking against sudden conversions.

The Lord goes to be the publican's guest, and while He is there the Pharisees began to murmur and complain. It would have been a good thing if Pharisees had died off with that generation; but, unfortunately, they have left a good many grandchildren, living down here in this nineteenth century, who are ever complaining, "This man receiveth *sinners*." But while the Pharisees were complaining, the Lord uttered the words of text: ' I did not come to Zaccheus to make him wretched, to condemn him, to torment him; I came to bless and save him. *The Son of Man is come to seek and to save that which was lost.*"

If there is a man or woman reading this who believes that he or she is *lost*, I have good news to tell you—Christ is come after you.

I was at the Fulton Street prayer-meeting one Saturday night a good many years ago, and when the meeting was over, a man came to me, and said, "I would like to have you go down to the city prison to-morrow, and preach to the prisoners." I said I would be very glad to go. There was no chapel in connection with that prison, and I was to preach to them in their cells. I had to stand at a little iron railing and talk down a great, long, narrow passage way to some three or four hundred of them, I suppose, all out of sight. It was pretty difficult work; I never preached to bare walls before. When it was over I thought I would like to see to whom I had been preaching, and how they had received the gospel. I went to the first door, where the inmates could have heard me best, and looked in at a little window, and there were some men playing cards; I suppose they had been playing all the while. " How is it with you here? " I said. "Well, stranger, we don't

want you to get a bad idea of us. False witnesses swore
a lie, and that is how we are here." "Oh," I said,
"Christ cannot save anybody here; there is nobody
lost." I went to the next cell. "Well, friend, how is
it with you?" "Oh," said the prisoner, "the man that
did the deed looked very much like me, so they canght
me and I am here." He was innocent, too. I passed
along to the next cell. "How is it with you?" "Well,
we got into bad company, and the man that did it got
clear, and we got taken up, but we never did anything."
I went along to the next cell. "How is it with you?"
"Our trial comes on next week, but they have nothing
against us, and we'll get free." I went round nearly
every cell, but the answer was always the same—they
had never done anything. Why, I never saw so many
innocent men together in my life! There was nobody
to blame but the magistrates, according to their way of
it. These men were wrapping their filthy rags of self-
righteousness about them. And that has been the story
for six thousand years.

I got discouraged as I went through the prison, on,
and on, and on, cell after cell, and every man had an
excuse. If he hadn't one, the devil helped him to make
one.

I had got almost through the prison, when I came to
a cell and found a man with his elbows on his knees,
and his head in his hands. Two little streams of tears
were running down his cheeks; they did not come by
drops that time.

"What's the trouble?" I said. He looked up, the
picture of remorse and despair. "Oh, my sins are
more than I can bear." "Thank God for that," I
replied. "What," said he, "you are the man that has

been preaching to us, ain't you?" "Yes." "I think
you said you were a *friend?*" "I am." "And yet you
are glad that my sins are more than I can bear!" "I
will explain," I said; "if your sins are more than you
can bear, won't you cast them on One who will bear
them for you?" "Who's that?" "The Lord Jesus."
"He won't bear *my* sins." "Why not?" "I have
sinned against Him all my life. "I don't care if you
have; the blood of Jesus Christ, God's Son, cleanses
from all sin." Then I told him how Christ had come to
seek and save that which was lost; to open the prison
doors and set the captives free. It was like a cup of
refreshment to find a man who believed he was lost, so
I stood there, and held up a crucified Savior to him.
" Christ was delivered for our offences, died for our sins,
rose again for our justification." For a long time the
man could not believe that such a miserable wretch
could be saved. He went on to enumerate his sins, and
I told him that the blood of Christ could cover them all.
After I had talked with him I said, " Now let us pray."
He got down on his knees inside the cell, and I knelt
outside. I said, " You pray." " Why," he said, " it
would be blasphemy for me to call on God." " You
call on God," I said. He knelt down, and, like the poor
publican, he lifted up his voice and said, " God be
merciful to me, a vile wretch!" I put my hand through
the window, and as I shook hands with him a tear that
burned down into my soul fell on my hand. It was a
tear of repentance. He believed he was lost. Then I
tried to get him to believe that Christ had come to save
him. I left him still in darkness. "I will be at the
hotel," I said, "between nine and ten o'clock, and I will
pray for you." Next morning, I felt so much interested

in him that I thought I must see him before I went back to Chicago. No sooner had my eye lighted on his face than I saw that remorse and despair had fled away. His countenance was beaming with celestial light; the tears of joy had come into his eyes, and the tears of despair were gone. The Sun of Righteousness had broken out across his path: his soul was leaping within him for joy; he had received Christ, as Zaccheus did, joyfully. "Tell me about it," I said. "Well, I do not know what time it was; I think it was about midnight. I had been in distress a long time, when all at once my great burden fell off, and now I believe I am the happiest man in New York." I think he was the happiest man I saw from the time I left Chicago till I got back again. His face was lighted up with the light that comes from the celestial hills. I bade him good-bye, and I expect to meet him in another world.

Can you tell me why the Son of God came down to that prison that night, and, passing cell after cell, went to that one, and set the captive free? It was

BECAUSE THE MAN BELIEVED HE WAS LOST.

O that we would wake up to the thought of what it is to be lost! The world has been rocked to sleep by Satan, who is going up and down and telling people that it doesn't mean anything. I believe in the old-fashioned heaven and hell. Christ came down to save us from a terrible hell, and any man who is cast down to hell from here must go in the full blaze of the gospel, and over the mangled body of the Son of God.

We hear of a man who has lost his health, and we sympathize with him, and we say it is very sad. Our hearts are drawn out in sympathy. Here is another man who has lost his wealth, and we say, "That is very sad." Here is another man who has lost his reputation, his standing among men. "That is sadder still," you say. We know what it is to lose health and wealth and reputation, but what is the loss of all these things compared with the loss of the soul?

I was in an eye-infirmary in Chicago some time before the great fire. A mother brought a beautiful little babe to the doctor—a babe only a few months old,—and wanted the doctor to look at the child's eyes. He did so, and pronounced it blind—blind for life—it would never see again. The moment he said that, the mother seized it, pressed it to her bosom, and gave a terrible scream. It pierced my heart, and I could not but weep; the doctor wept; we could not help it. "Oh, my darling," she said, "are you never to see the mother that gave you birth? Oh, doctor, I cannot stand it. My child, my child!" It was a sight to move any heart. But what is the loss of eyesight to the loss of a soul? I had a thousand times rather have these eyes taken out of my head and go to the grave blind, than lose my soul. I have two sons and no one but God knows how I love them; but I would see their eyes dug out of their heads rather than see them grow up to manhood and go down to the grave without Christ and without hope. The loss of a soul! Christ knew what it meant. That is what brought Him from the bosom of the Father; that is what brought Him from the throne; that is what brought Him to Calvary. The Son of God was in earnest. When He died on Calvary it was to save a lost world; it was to save your soul and mine.

O the loss of the soul—how terrible it is! If you are still lost I beseech you do not rest until you have found peace in Christ. Fathers and mothers, if you have children out of the Ark, do not rest until they are brought into it. Do not discourage your children from coming to Christ. The Son of man came to save children as much as old grey-haired men. He came for all, rich and poor, young and old. Young man, if you are lost may God show it to you, and may you press into the kingdom. The Son of man is come to seek and to save you.

There is a story told of Rowland Hill. He was once preaching in the open air to a vast audience. Lady Anne Erskine was riding by, and she asked who it was that was addressing the vast assembly. She was told that it was the celebrated Rowland Hill. Said she, "I have heard of him; drive me near the platform, that I may listen to him." The eye of Rowland Hill rested on her. He saw that she belonged to the aristocracy, and turning to some one, he inquired who she was. He went on preaching, and all at once he stopped. "My friends," he said, "I have got something here for sale." Everybody was startled to think that a minister was going to sell something in his sermon. "I am going to sell it by auction, and it is worth more than the crown of all Europe, it is the soul of Lady Anne Erskine. Will any one bid for her soul? Hark! methinks I hear a bid. Who bids? Satan bids. What will you give? I will give riches, honor, and pleasure; yea, I will give the whole world for her soul. Hark! I hear another bid for this soul. Who bids? The Lord Jesus Christ. Jesus, what will you give for this soul? I will give peace, and joy, and comfort that the world knows not of; yea, I will give eternal life for her soul." Turning to Lady Anne Erskine he said,

"You have heard the two bidders for your soul—which shall have it?" She ordered the footman to open the door, and pushing her way through the crowd, she said, "The Lord Jesus shall have my soul, if He will accept it."

That story may be true, or it may not; but there is one thing I *know* to be true—there are two bidders for your soul now. It is for you to decide which shall have it. Satan offers you what he cannot give; he is a liar, and has been from the foundation of the world. I pity the man who is living on the devil's promises. He lied to Adam, deceived him, stripped him of all he had, and then left him in his lost, ruined condition. And all the men since Adam, living on the devil's lies, the devil's promises, have been disappointed, and will be, down to the end of the chapter. But the Lord Jesus Christ is able to give all He offers, and He offers eternal life to every lost soul. The gift of God is eternal life. Who will have it? Will any one flash it over the wires, and let it go up to the throne of God, that you want to be saved?

Some time since a man told me he was anxious to be saved, but Christ had never sought for him. I said, "What are you waiting for?" "Why," he said, "I am waiting for Christ to call me. As soon as He calls me, I am coming." There may be others here who have got the same notion. Now I do not believe there is a man in this land that the Spirit of God has not striven with at some period of his life. I do not believe there is a person but Christ has sought after him. Bear in mind, He takes the place of the seeker. Every man who has ever been saved through these six thousand years was first sought after by God. No sooner did Adam fall, than God sought him. He had gone away frightened, and hid himself among the bushes in the garden, but God took the place of the seeker; and from that day to this God has always had the place of the seeker. No man or woman has ever been saved but that He sought them first.

What do we read in the fifteenth chapter of St. Luke? There is a shepherd bringing home his sheep into the fold. As they pass in, he stands and numbers them. I can see him counting one, two, three, up to ninety-nine. "But," says he, "I ought to have a hundred. I must have made a mistake"; and he counts them over again. "There are only ninety-nine here. I must have lost one." He does not say, "I will let him find his own way back." No! He takes the place of the seeker. He goes out into the mountain, and hunts until he finds the lost one, and then he lays it on his shoulder and brings it home. Is it the sheep that finds the shepherd? No, it is the shepherd that finds and brings back the sheep. He rejoiced to find it. Undoubtedly the sheep was very glad to get back to the fold, but it was the shepherd who rejoiced, and who called his friends and said, "Rejoice with me."

Then there is that woman who lost the piece of money. Some one perhaps had paid her a bill that day, giving her ten pieces of silver. As she retires at night, she takes the money out of her pocket and counts it. "Why," she says, "I have only got nine pieces. I ought to have ten." She counts it over again. "Only nine pieces! Where have I been since I got that money? I am sure I have not been out of the house." She turns her pocket wrong side out, and there she finds a hole in it. Does she wait until the money gets back into her pocket? No. She takes a broom, and lights a candle, and sweeps diligently. She moves the sofa and the table and the chairs, and all the rest of the furniture, and sweeps in every corner until she finds it. And when she has found it, who rejoices? The piece of money? No; the woman who finds it. In these parables, Christ brings out the great truth that God takes the place of seeker. People talk of finding Christ, but it is Christ who first finds them.

Another young man told me one night that he was too great a sinner to be saved. Why, they are the very men Christ came after. "This Man receiveth sinners and eateth with them." The only charge they could bring against Christ down here was that He was receiving bad men. They are the very kind He is willing to receive. All you have got to do is to prove that you are a sinner, and I will prove that you have got a Savior. And the greater the sinner, the greater need you have of a Savior. You say your heart is hard; well, then, of course, you want Christ to soften it. You cannot do it yourself. The harder your heart, the more need you have of Christ; the blacker you are, the more need you have of a Savior. If your sins rise up before you like a dark mountain, bear in mind that the blood of Jesus Christ cleanses from all sin. There is no sin so big, or so black, or so corrupt and vile, but the blood of Christ can cover it. So I preach the old gospel again, "The Son of Man is come to seek and to save that which was lost."

It was Adam's fall, his *loss*, that brought out God's love. God never told Adam, when He put him into Eden, that He loved him. It was his fall, his sin, that brought it out. A friend of mine from Manchester was in Chicago a few years ago, and he was very much interested in the city—a great city, with its 300,000 or 400,000 inhabitants, with its great railway centers, its lumber market, its pork market, and its grain market. He said he went back to Manchester and told his friends about Chicago. But he could not get anybody very much interested in it. It was a great many hundreds of miles away, and the people did not seem to care for hearing about it. But one day there came flashing along the wire the sad tidings that it was on fire; and, my friend said, the Manchester people became suddenly interested in Chicago! Every despatch that came they read. They bought up the papers, and devoured every particle of news. And at last, when the despatch came that Chicago was burning up, that 100,000 people were turned out of house and home, then every one became so interested that they began to weep for us. They came forward and laid down their money—some gave hundreds of dollars for the relief of the poor sufferers. It was the *calamity* of Chicago that brought out the love of Manchester, and of London, and of Liverpool. I was in that terrible fire, and I saw men that were wealthy stripped of all they had. That Sunday night, when they retired, they were the richest men in Chicago. Next morning they were paupers. I did not see a man weep. But when the news came flashing along the wire, "Liverpool gives ten thousand dollars; Manchester sends five thousand dollars; London is giving money to aid the city"; as the news kept flashing that help was coming, our city was broken-hearted. I saw men weep then. The love that was shown us broke our hearts. So the love of God ought to break every heart to-day. It was love that brought Christ down here to

die for us. It was love that made Him leave His place by the Father's throne and come down here *to seek and to save that which was lost.*

But now for the sake of these men who believe Christ never sought them, perhaps it would be well to say *how* He seeks. There are a great many ways in which He does so.

One night I found a man in the inquiry-room, and the Lord had been speaking to him by the prayers of a godly sister who died a little while ago. Her prayers were answered. He came into the inquiry-room trembling from head to foot. I talked to him about the plan of salvation, and the tears trickled down his cheeks, and at last he took Christ as his Savior. The Son of Man sought out that young man through the prayers of his sister, and then through her death.

Some of you have godly, praying mothers, who have prayed whole nights for your soul, and who have now gone to heaven. Did not you take their hand and promise that you would meet them there? That was the Son of God seeking you by your mother's prayers and your mother's death. Some of you have got faithful, godly ministers who weep for you in the pulpit, and plead with you to come to Christ. You have heard heart-searching sermons, and the truth has gone down deep into your heart, and tears have come down your cheeks. That was the Son of God seeking you. Some of you have had godly, praying Sabbath-school teachers and superintendents, urging you to come to Christ. Some of you, perhaps, have got young men converted around you, and they have talked with you and pleaded with you to come to Christ. That was the Son of God seeking after your soul. Some of you have had a tract put into your hand with the startling title, "Eternity; Where will you spend it?" and the arrow has gone home. That was the Son of God seeking after you. Many of you have been laid on a bed of sickness, when you had time to think and meditate, and in the silent watches of the night, when everybody was asleep, the Spirit of God has come into your chamber, has come to your bedside, and the thought came stealing through your mind that you ought to be a child of God and an heir of heaven. That was the Son of God seeking after your lost soul. Some of you have had little children, and you have laid them in the cemetery. When that little child was dying you promised to love and serve God. Ah, have you kept your promise? That was the Son of God seeking you. He took that little child yonder to draw your affections heavenwards. .

O friends, open the door of your heart and let the heavenly Visitor in. Do not turn Him away any longer. Do not say with Felix, "Go Thy way this time, and when I have a convenient season I will call for Thee." Make this a convenient season; make this the hour of your salvation. Receive the gift of God now, open the door of your heart, and say: "Welcome, thrice welcome into this heart of mine."

V.

SINNERS SEEKING CHRIST.

"SEEK THE LORD WHILE HE MAY BE FOUND; CALL YE
UPON HIM WHILE HE IS NEAR."—ISAIAH LV. 6.

I have been speaking about the Son of Man seeking
the lost, but now I want to take up the other side of the
case—man's side. I have learned this, that when any
one becomes in earnest about his soul's salvation he begins to seek God, and it does not take a great while for
them to meet; it does not take long for an anxious sinner to meet an anxious Savior.

What do we read in the 29th chapter of Jeremiah,
13th verse? "Ye shall seek me and find me when ye
shall search for me *with all your heart*." These are the
men who find Christ—those who seek for Him with all
their heart. I am tired and sick of half-heartedness.
You don't like a half-hearted man, you don't care for
any one to love you with a half-heart; and the Lord
won't have it. If we are going to seek for Him and find
Him, we must do it with all our heart. I believe the
reason why so few people find Christ is because they do
not search for Him with all their heart; they are not
terribly in earnest about their soul's salvation. *God* is
in earnest; everything God has done proves that He is
in earnest about the salvation of men's souls. He has
proved it by giving His only Son to die for us. The
Son of God was in earnest when He died. What is

Calvary but a proof of that? And the Lord wants us to be in earnest when it comes to this great question of the soul's salvation. I never saw men seeking Him with all their hearts but they soon found Him.

It was quite refreshing, one night, to find in the inquiry-room a young man who thought he was not worth saving, he was so vile and wicked. There was hope for him because he was so desperately in earnest about his soul. He thought he was worthless. He had got a sight of himself in God's looking-glass, and when a man does that he has a very poor opinion of himself. You can always tell when a man is a great way from God—he is always talking about himself, and how good he is. But the moment he sees God by the eye of faith he is down on his knees, and, like Job, he cries, "Behold, I am vile." All his goodness flees away. What men want is to be in earnest about their salvation, and they will soon find Christ. You do not need to go up to the heights to bring Him down, or down to the depths to bring Him up, or to go off to some distant city to find Him. This day He is near to every one of us. I once heard some one in the inquiry-room telling a young person to go home and seek Christ in his closet. I would not dare to tell any one to do that. You might be dead before you got home. If I read my Bible correctly, the man who preaches the gospel is not the man who tells me to seek Christ to-morrow or an hour hence, but *now.* He is near to every one of us this minute to save. If the world would just come to God for salvation, and be in earnest about it, they would find the Son of God right at the door of their heart.

Suppose I should say I have lost a very valuable dia-mond here,—worth $100,000. I had it in my pocket when I came into the hall, and when I had done preaching I found it was not in my pocket, but was in the hall somewhere. Suppose I should say that any one who finds it could have it. How earnest you would all become! You would not get very much of my sermon; you would all be thinking of the diamond. I do not believe the police could get you out of this hall. The idea of finding a diamond worth $100,000! If you could only find it, it would lift you out of poverty at once, and you would be independent for the rest of your days. Oh, how soon everybody would become terribly in earnest then!

I would to God I could get men to seek for Christ in the same way. I have got something worth more than a diamond to offer you. Is not salvation—eternal life— worth more than all the diamonds in the world?

People seem to sleep, and to forget that there is no door out of hell. If they enter there they must remain, age after age. Millions on millions of years will roll on, but there will be no door, no escape out of hell. May God wake you up and make you anxious about your soul. People talk about our being earnest and fanatical —about our being on fire. Would to God the Church was on fire! This world would soon shake to its foundation. May God wake up a slumbering Church! What we want men to do is not to shout "Amen," and clasp their hands. The deepest and quietest waters very often run swiftest. We want men to go right to work; there will be a chance for them to shout by-and-by. Go and speak to your neighbor, and tell him of Christ and heaven. You need not go far before you will find some one who is passing down to the darkness of eternal death. Let us haste to the rescue!

What we want to see is men really wishing to become
Christians, men who are in dead earnest about it. The
idea of hearing a man say in answer to the question,
"Do you want to become a Christian?" "Well, I *would
not mind*." My friend, I do not think *you* will ever get
into the kingdom of God until you change your language. We want men crying from the depths of their
heart, "I *want* to be saved." On the day of Pentecost
the cry was, "Men and brethren, what shall we do?"
These men were in earnest, and they found Christ right
there; three thousand found Him, when they sought
with all their hearts. When men seek Christ as they
do wealth, they will soon find Him. To be sure, the
world will raise a cry that they are excited. Let cotton
go up ten or fifteen per cent. before to-morrow morning,
and you will see how quickly the merchants will get
excited! And the papers don't cry it down either.
They say it is healthy excitement; commerce is getting
on. But when you begin to get excited about your
soul's salvation, and are in earnest, then they raise the
cry, "Oh, they are getting excited; most unhealthy
state of things." Yet they don't talk about men hastening down to death by thousands. There is the poor
drunkard, look at him! Hear the piercing cry going up
to heaven? Yet the Church of God slumbers and sleeps.
Here and there there is an inquirer, and yet they go into
the inquiry-room as if they were half-asleep. When
will men seek for Christ as they seek for wealth, or as
they seek for honor?

As I have said, if life is in danger, how terribly in
earnest men become. That is right; there is no doubt
about *that*. But why should not men be as much in
earnest about their soul's salvation? Why should not

every man and woman wake up and seek the Lord with all their heart? Then, the Lord says, you *shall* find Him.

There is a story told of a vessel that was wrecked, and was going down at sea. There were not enough lifeboats to take all on board. When the vessel went down, some of the lifeboats were near the vessel. A man swam from the wreck, just as it was going down, to one of the boats; but they had no room to take him, and they refused. When they refused, he seized hold of the boat with his right hand; but they took a sword and cut off his fingers. When he had lost the fingers of his right hand, the man was so earnest to save his life that he seized the boat with his left hand; they cut off the fingers of that hand too. Then the man swam up and seized the boat with his teeth, and they had compassion on him and relented. They could not cut off his head, so they took him in, and the man saved his life. Why? *Because he was in earnest.* Why not seek your soul's salvation as that man sought to save his life?

Will there ever be

A BETTER TIME?

Will there ever be a better time for the old man whose locks are growing grey, whose eyes are growing dim, and who is hastening to the grave? Is not this the very best time for him? "Seek the Lord *while He may be found.*" There is a man in the middle of life. Is this not the best time for *him* to seek the kingdom of God? Will he ever have a better opportunity? Will Christ ever be more willing to save than now? He says, "Come, for *all* things are now ready." Not "*going to bc*," but "are *now* ready." There is a young man. My friend, is it not the best time for you to seek the king- dom of God? Seek the Lord, you can find Him now. Can you say that you will find Him to-morrow? Young man, you know not what to-morrow may bring forth. Do you know that every time the clock ticks, a soul passes away? Is not this the best time for you to seek the kingdom of God? My boy, the Lord wants *you*. Seek first the kingdom of God, and seek Him while He may be found.

About thirty years ago, a great revival swept over this land. A great many men stood and shook their heads; they could not believe it was a healthy state of things. The Church was not in its normal state! The Church from Maine to Minnesota, and on to California, was astir. As you passed over this great republic, over its western prairies and mountains, and through its valleys, as you went on by train, passing through its cities and vil- lages, you could see the churches lit up; and men were flocking into the kingdom of God by hundreds. In a year and a half or two years there were more than half a million souls brought in. Men said it was false ex- citement, wildfire, and it would pass away. But, my friend, it was grace preceding judgment. Little did we know that our nation was soon to be baptized in blood, and that we would soon hear the tramp of a million men, that hundreds and thousands of our young men, the flower of our nation, would soon be lying in a sol- dier's grave. But, oh, my friend, it was God calling His people in. He was preparing our nation for a ter- rible struggle.

Supposing you could win the world, what would you do with it? Would it be worth as much as Christ?

Let everything else be laid aside, and make up your minds that you will not rest until you have sought and found the Lord Jesus. I never knew any one make up his mind to seek Him but He soon found Him.

At Dublin a young man found Christ. He went home and lived so godly and so Christlike a life that two of his brothers could not understand what had wrought the change in him. They left Dublin and followed us to Sheffield, and found Christ there. They were in earnest. But, thanks be to God, Christ can be found now. I firmly believe every reader can find Christ now, if you will seek for Him with all your heart. He says, "Call upon me." Did you ever hear of any one calling upon Christ with the whole heart, that Christ didn't answer? Look at that thief on the cross! It may have been that he had a praying mother, and that his mother taught him the fifty-third chapter of Isaiah. He had heard Christ pray that wonderful prayer, "Father, forgive them." And as he was hanging on the cross that text of Scripture came to his mind, "Seek ye the Lord while He may be found; call ye upon Him while He is near." The truth came flashing into his soul, and he said, "He is near me now. I will call on Him. Lord, remember me when Thou comest into Thy kingdom." No sooner had he called than the Lord said, "This day shalt thou be with me in paradise." That was his seeking opportunity, his day. My friend, this is your day now. I believe that every man has his day. You have it just now; why not call upon Him just now? Say, as the poor thief did, "Lord, remember me." That was his golden opportunity, and the Lord heard and answered and saved him. Did not Bartimeus call on Him while He was near? Christ was passing by Jericho for the last time, and he cried out, "Thou Son of David, have mercy on me." And did not the Lord hear his prayer, and give him sight? It was a good thing Zaccheus called—or rather the Lord called him, but when the Lord called he came. May the Lord call you, and may you respond, "Lord, here am I; you have called, and I come." Do you believe the Lord will call a poor sinner, and then cast him out? No! His Word stands forever, "Him that cometh to me I will in no wise cast out."

I was glad when that man I told you of, said he felt as if he was too bad. Men are pretty near the kingdom of God when they do not see anything good in themselves. At the Fulton Street prayer-meeting a man came in, and this was his story. He said he had a mother who prayed for him; he was a wild, reckless prodigal. Some time after his mother's death he began to be troubled. He thought he ought to get into new company, and leave his old companions, so he said he would go and join a secret society. He thought he would join the Odd Fellows. They made inquiry about him, and found he was a drunken sailor, so they black-balled him. They would not have him. He went to the Freemasons. He had nobody to recommend him, so they inquired and found there was no good in his character, and they black-balled him. They didn't want him. One day, some one handed him a little notice in the street about the prayer-meeting, and he went in. He heard that Christ had come to save sinners. He believed Him; he took Him at His word; and, in reporting the matter, he said he "*came to Christ without a character, and Christ hadn't black-balled him.*"

My friend, that is Christ's way. Are you without a

character, with nobody to say a good word for you? I bring you good news. Call on the Son of God, and He will hear you. Call on Him now.

My friend, let us be in earnest about the salvation of our children, and of our friends. Warn that young lady. Yes, mother, speak to that daughter of yours. Father, speak to that child of yours. Wife, speak to your unconverted husband. Husband, speak to your unconverted wife. Do not let any one say, "Nobody cares for my soul." I never saw a mother burdened for her children but they soon became anxious.

Before I close, I want to ask you once more, What are you going to do? If the Lord is near, won't you call upon Him? Don't let some scoffer keep you out of the kingdom of God. There may be a scornful look upon his face; perhaps he makes light of what I say. Don't mind him; don't look to him; but look right up to God, and ask Him to save you. Every true friend, if you could get his advice, would tell you to be saved now. Ask your minister, "Had I better seek the kingdom of God now?" What does he tell you? "By all means, don't put it off another minute." Ask your godly praying mother, "Is it best to seek the kingdom of God now?" Does she say, "Put it off one week, or put it off one month"? Do you think your mother would say that? There is not a Christian mother in this land who would say it. I doubt if there is an unconverted mother even whose advice would be to put off becoming a Christian. Ask that praying sister of yours, ask that praying brother, ask any friend you have whether it is not the very best thing you can do. And then cry to heaven and ask Him who is sitting at the right hand of God, and who loves you more than your father or your mother, or anyone on earth—who loves you so much that He gave Himself for you—ask *Him* what He will have you do, and hear His voice from the throne, "Seek first the kingdom of God." And then shout down to the infernal regions, and ask those down there, and what will they say? "Send someone to my father's house, for I have five brethren, that he may testify unto them, lest they also come into this place." Heaven, earth, and hell unite in this one thing, "Seek first the kingdom of God." Don't put it off. Call upon Him while He is near. And if you call upon Him in real earnest He will hear that call.

You may call

TOO LATE.

I have no doubt that those who would not pray when the ark was building prayed when the flood came, but their prayer was not answered. I have no doubt that when Lot went out of Sodom, Sodom cried to God, but it was too late, and God's judgment swept them from the earth. My friend, it is not too late now, but it may be at twelve o'clock to-night. I cannot find any place in the Bible where I can say you may call to-morrow. I am not justified in saying that. "Behold NOW is the accepted time, NOW is .the day of salvation." Those men of Jerusalem, what a golden opportunity they had, with Christ in their midst! We see the Son of God weeping over Jerusalem, His heart bursting with grief for the city as He cried, "O Jerusalem, Jerusalem! thou that stonest the prophets, how often would I have gathered thee as a hen gathereth her brood, but ye would not." He could look down forty years. and see Titus coming with his army, and besieging that city

They called upon God then, but it was too late, and eleven hundred thousand people perished. Now is a time of mercy. It may be I am talking to some one whose days of grace may be few, to some one who may be snatched away very soon, who may never hear another gospel sermon, who may be hearing *the last call.* My friend, be wise! Make up your mind that you will seek the kingdom of God now. " Behold, now is the accepted time: behold now is the day of salvation." Christ is inviting you to come—"Come unto me, all ye that labor and are heavy-laden, and I will give you rest." Oh, may we all find rest in Christ now! Do not let anything divert your mind, but make up your mind this hour that you will settle this great question of eternity.

WHAT THINK YE OF CHRIST?

MATT. XXII. 42.

I suppose no one is reading this who has not thought more or less about Christ. You have heard about Him, and heard men preach about Him. For nearly nineteen hundred years men have been talking about Him, and thinking about Him. Some have their minds made up about Him, who He is, and doubtless some have not. And although all these years have rolled away, this question comes up, addressed to each of us, to-day:

"What think ye of Christ?"

I do not know why it should not be thought a proper question for one man to put to another. If I were to ask you what you think of any prominent public man, you would already have your mind made up about him. If I were to ask you what you think of the President, you would speak right out and tell me your opinion in a minute. If I were to ask about the secretary of state, you would tell me freely what you had for or against him. And why should not people make up their minds about the Lord Jesus Christ, and take their stand for or against Him? If you think well of Him, why not speak well of Him, and range yourselves on His side? And if you think ill of Him, and believe Him to be an impostor, and that He did not die to save the world, why not lift up your voice, and say you are against Him? It would be a happy day for Christianity if men would just take sides—if we could know positively who was really for Him, and who was against Him.

It is of very little importance what the world thinks of any one else. Kings and princes, presidents and generals must soon be gone. Yes, it matters little, comparatively, what we think of them. Their lives can only interest a few; but every living soul on the face of the earth is concerned with this Man. The question for the world is, "What think ye of Christ?" I do not ask you what you think of the Episcopal Church, or of the Presbyterians, or the Baptists, or the Roman Catholics; I do not ask you what you think of this minister or that, of this doctrine of that; but I want to ask you what you think of the living person, Jesus Christ?

I should like to ask, was He really the Son of God—the great God-man? Did He leave heaven and come down to this world for a purpose? Was it really to seek and to save? I should like to begin with the manger, and follow Him up through the thirty-three years He was here upon earth. I should like to ask you what you think of His coming into this world, and being born in a manger when it might have been a palace; why He left the grandeur and glory of heaven, and the royal retinue of angels; why He passed by palaces and crowns and dominion, and came down here alone?

I should like to ask what you think of Him as *a teacher*. He spake as never man spake. I should like to take Him up as *a preacher*. I should like to bring you to that mountain side that we might listen to the words as they fall from His gentle lips. Talk about the preachers of the present day! I would rather a thousand times be five minutes at the feet of Christ than listen a lifetime to all the wise men in the world!

I should like to ask you what you think of Him as a *physician*. A man would soon have a reputation as a doctor if he could cure as Christ did. No case was ever brought to Him but He was a match for it. He had but to speak the word, and disease fled before Him. Here comes a man covered with leprosy. "Lord, if Thou wilt Thou canst make me clean," he cries. "I will," says the great Physician, and in an instant the leprosy is gone. The world has hospitals for incurable diseases, but there were no incurable diseases with Him.

Now see Him in the little home at Bethany, binding up the wounded hearts of Martha and Mary, and tell me what you think of Him as a *comforter*. He is a husband to the widow, and a father to the fatherless. The weary may find a resting=place upon His breast, and the friendless may reckon Him their friend. He never varies, He never fails, He never dies. His sympathy is ever fresh, His love is ever free. O widow and orphans, O sorrowing and mourning, will you not thank God for Christ the comforter?

But these are not the points I wish to take up now. Let us go to those who knew Christ, and ask what they thought of Him. If you want to find out what a man is now=a=days, inquire about him from those who know him best. I do not wish to be partial; we will go to Christ's enemies and friends. We will ask His friends and His enemies, What think ye of Christ? If we only went to those who liked Him, you would say, "Oh, he is so blind; he thinks so much of the man that he can't see his faults. You can't get anything out of him, unless it be in his favor; it is a one=sided affair alto.gether." So we shall go in the first place to His enemies, to those who hated Him, persecuted Him, cursed and slew Him. I shall put you in the jury-box, and call upon them to tell us what they think of Him.

I.

First, among the witnesses, let us call upon *the Pharisees*. We know how they hated Him. Let us put a few questions to them.

Come, Pharisees, tell us what you have against the Son of God! What do *you* think of Christ?

Hear what they say! *"This man receiveth sinners."*

What an argument to bring against Him! Why, it is the very thing that makes us love Him! It is the glory of the gospel. He receives sinners. If He had not, what would have become of *us?* Have you nothing more to bring against Him than *this?* Why, it is one of the greatest compliments that was ever paid Him!

Once more: when He was hanging on the tree, you had this to say of Him, "He saved others, Himself He cannot save." And so He died to save others, but He could not save Himself and save us too? He laid down His own life for yours and mine. Yes, Pharisees, you have told the truth for once in your lives! *He saved others.* He died for others. He was a ransom for many; so it is quite true what you think of Him—"*He saved others, Himself He cannot save.*"

Now, let us call upon *Caiaphas*. Let him stand up here in his flowing robes; let us ask him for his evidence.

Caiaphas, you were chief priest when Christ was tried. You were president of the Sanhedrim. You were in the council-chamber when they found Him guilty. You yourself condemned Him. Tell us; what did the witnesses say? On what grounds did you judge Him? What testimony was brought against Him?

"He hath spoken blasphemy," says Caiaphas. "He said, 'Hereafter shall ye see the Son of man sitting on the right hand of power, and coming in the clouds of heaven.' When I heard that, I found Him guilty of blasphemy, I rent my mantle, and condemned Him to death."

Yes, all that they had against Him was that He was the Son of God; and they slew Him for the promise of His coming for His bride.

Now, let us summon *Pilate.* Let him enter the witness-box.

Pilate, this man was brought before you. You examined Him. You talked with Him face to face. What think *you* of Christ?

"I find no fault in Him," says Pilate. "He said He was the King of the Jews," (just as he wrote it over the cross), "but I find no fault in Him."

Such is the testimony of the man who examined Him! And as he stands there, the center of a Jewish mob, there comes along a man, elbowing his way, in haste. He rushes up to Pilate, and thrusting out his hand, gives him a message. He tears it open; his face turns pale as he reads—"Have thou nothing to do with *this just man,* for I have suffered many things this day in a dream because of Him." It is from *Pilate's wife*—her testimony to Christ. You want to know what His enemies thought of Him? You want to know what a heathen thought? Well, here it is, "no fault in Him"; and the wife of a heathen, "this just man"!

And now, look—in comes *Judas.* He ought to make a good witness. Let us address him.

Come tell us, Judas, what think *you* of Christ? You knew the Master well. You sold Him for thirty pieces of silver. You betrayed Him with a kiss. You saw Him perform those miracles. You were with Him in Jerusalem. In Bethany, when He summoned Lazarus from the dead, you were there. What think you of Him?

I can see him as he comes into the presence of the chief priests; I can hear the money ring as he dashes it upon the table—"*I have betrayed innocent blood!*" Here is the man who betrayed Him, and this is what he thinks of Him!

Yes my friend, God has made every man who had anything to do with the death of His Son put their tesimony on record that He was an innocent Man.

Let us take *the Centurion,* who was present at the execution. He had charge of the Roman soldiers. He had told them to make Him carry His cross. He had given orders for the nails to be driven into His feet and hands, for the spear to be thrust in His side. Let the Centurion come forward.

"Centurion, you had charge of the executioners. You saw that the order for His death was carried out. You saw Him die. You heard Him speak upon the cross. Tell us, *what think you of Christ?*"

Hark! Look at him! He is smiting his breast as he cries, "*Truly, this was the Son of God!*"

I might go to *the thief on the cross,* and ask what he thought of Him. At first he railed upon Him and reviled Him. But then he thought better of it. "This man hath done nothing amiss," he said. I might go further. I might summon the very *devils* themselves and ask them for their testimony. Have *they* anything to say of Him? Why, the very devils called Him the Son of God! In Mark we have the unclean

spirit crying, "Jesus, Thou Son of the most High God."
Men say, "Oh, I believe Christ to be the Son of God,
and because I believe it intellectually, I shall be saved."
I tell you the devils did that. And they did more than
that, *they trembled*

II.

Let us now bring in His friends. We want you to
hear their evidence.

Let us first call that prince of preachers. Let us hear
the forerunner, the wilderness preacher, *John*. Save the
Master Himself, none ever preached like this man—this
man who drew all Jerusalem and all Judea into the
wilderness to hear him; this man who burst upon the
nations like the flash of a meteor. Let John the Baptist come with his leathern girdle and his hairy coat
and let him tell us what he thinks of Christ.

His words, though they were echoed in the wilderness
of Palestine, are written in the Book forever, "Behold
the Lamb of God which taketh away the sin of the
world." This is what John the Baptist thought of Him.
"I bare record that He is the Son of God." No wonder
he drew all Jerusalem and Judea to him, because he
preached Christ. And whenever men preach Christ,
they are sure to have plenty of followers.

Let us bring in *Peter*, who was with Him on the
Mount of Transfiguration, who was with Him the night
He was betrayed.

"Come, Peter, tell us what you think of Christ.
Stand in the witness-box and testify of Him. You de-
nied him once. You said, with a curse, you did not
know Him. Was it true, Peter? Don't you know
Him?"

"Know Him!" I can imagine Peter saying; "it was a lie I told them. I *did* know Him." Afterwards I can hear him charging home their guilt upon these Jerusalem sinners. He calls Him "both Lord and Christ." Such was his testimony on the day of Pentecost. "God hath made that same Jesus both Lord and Christ." And tradition tells us that when they came to execute Peter, he felt he was not worthy to die in the way his Master died, and he requested to be crucified with his head downwards. So much did Peter think of Him!

Now let us hear from the beloved disciple, *John*. He knew more about Christ than any other man. He had laid his head on his Savior's bosom. He had heard the throbbing of that loving heart. Look into his gospel if you wish to know what he thought of Him.

Matthew writes of Him as the Royal King come from His throne, Mark as the servant, and Luke as the Son of Man. John takes up his pen, and, with one stroke, forever settles the question of His divinity. He goes right back before the time of Adam. "In the beginning was the Word, and the Word was with God, and the word was God." Look into Revelation. He calls Him "the bright and the Morning Star." So John thought well of Him because he knew Him well.

We might bring in *Thomas*, the doubting disciple.

"You doubted Him, Thomas. You would not believe He had risen, and you put your fingers into the wound in His side. What do you think of Him?"

"*My Lord and my God!*" says Thomas.

Then go over to Decapolis and you will find Christ has been there casting out devils. Let us call the men of that country and ask what they think of Him. "*He hath done all things well,*" they say.

But we have other witnesses to bring in. Take the persecuting *Saul*, once one of the worst of His enemies. Breathing out threatenings, he meets Him. "Saul, Saul, why persecutest thou me?" says Christ; and He might have added, "What have I done to you? Have I injured you in any way? Did I not come to bless you? Why do you treat me thus, Saul?" And then Saul asks, "Who art Thou, Lord?" "I am Jesus of Nazareth, whom thou persecutest." You see, He was not ashamed of His name; although He had been in heaven, "I am *Jesus of Nazareth*." What a change did that one interview make in Saul! A few years after we hear him say, "I have suffered the loss of all things, and do count them but dross that I may win Christ." Such a testimony to the Savior!

But I shall go still further. I shall go away from earth into the other world. I shall summon the *angels* and ask what they think of Christ. They saw Him in the bosom of the Father before the world was. Before the dawn of creation, before the morning stars sang together, He was there. They saw Him leave the throne and come down to the manger. What a scene for them to witness! Ask these heavenly beings what they thought of Him then. For once they are permitted to speak; for once the silence of heaven is broken. Listen to their songs on the plains of Bethlehem, "Behold, I bring you good tidings of great joy, which shall be to all people, for unto you is born this day, in the city of David, a Savior, which is Christ the Lord." He leaves the throne to save the world. Is it a wonder the angels thought well of Him?

Then there are *the redeemed saints*—they that see Him face to face. Here on earth He was never known, no one seemed really to be acquainted with Him; but He was known in that world where He had been from the foundation. What do they think of Him there?

If we could hear from heaven, we should hear a shout which would glorify and magnify His name. We are told that when John was in the Spirit on the Lord's-day, and being caught up, he heard a shout around him, ten thousand times ten thousand, and thousands and thousands of voices, "Worthy is the Lamb that was slain, to receive power, and riches, and wisdom, and strength, and honor, and glory, and blessing!"

Yes, He is worthy of all this. Heaven cannot speak too well of Him. Oh that earth would take up the echo, and join with heaven in singing, "WORTHY to receive power, and riches, and wisdom, and strength, and honor, and glory, and blessing!"

But there is yet another witness, a higher still. Some think that the Jehovah of the Old Testament is the Christ of the New. But when Jesus came out of Jordan, baptized by John, there came a voice from heaven. God the Father spoke. It was His testimony to Christ: "This is my beloved Son, in whom I am well pleased."

Ah, yes! God the Father thinks well of the Son. And if God is well pleased with Him, so ought we to be. If the sinner and God are well pleased with Christ, then the sinner and God can meet. The moment you say as the Father said, "I am well pleased with Him," and accept Him, you are wedded to God. Will you not believe this witness, this last of all, the Lord of hosts, the King of kings, Himself? Once more He repeats it, so that all may know it. To Peter and James and John, on the mount of transfiguration, He says again, "This is my beloved Son; hear Him." And that voice went echoing and reechoing through Palestine, through all the earth from sea to sea; yes, that voice is echoing still. ' *Hear Him! Hear Him!* ' "

My friend, will you hear Him now? Hark! what is He saying to you? "Come unto me, all ye that labor and are heavy=laden, and I will give you rest. Take my yoke upon you and learn of me; for I am meek and lowly in heart; and ye shall find rest unto your souls. For my yoke is easy, and my burden is light." Will you not think well of such a Savior? Will you not believe in Him? Will you not trust in Him with all your heart and mind? Will you not live for Him? If He laid down His life for us, is it not the least we can do to lay down ours for Him? If He bore the cross and died on it for me, ought I not be willing to take it up for Him? Oh, have we not reason to think well of Him? Do you think it is right and noble to lift up your voice against such a Savior? Do you think it is just to cry, "Crucify Him! crucify Him!"?

Oh, may God help all of us to glorify the Father by thinking well of His only=begotten Son.

VII.

EXCUSES.

PART I.

" And they all with one consent began to make excuse. The first said unto him, I have bought a piece of ground, and I must needs go and see it: I pray thee have me excused. And another said, I have bought five yoke of oxen, and I go to prove them: I pray thee have me excused. And another said, I have married a wife, and therefore I cannot come."—*Luke xiv. 18-20.*

No sooner does anyone begin to preach the gospel than men and women begin to "make excuse." It is the old story. There is not an unsaved person but has got some excuse. If I were to go to each of you and ask why you do not accept God's invitation to the gospel feast, you would have an excuse ready on the end of your tongue; and if you had not one ready, the devil would be there to help you to make one. And if they could be answered, he is ready to make new ones. He has had six thousand years experience, and he is very good at it; he can give you as many as you want.

Do you know

THE ORIGIN OF EXCUSES?

You will find it away back in Eden. When Adam had sinned, he tried to excuse himself. "The woman *whom Thou gavest* to be with me, she gave me of the tree, and I did eat." He tried to lay all the blame on God; Eve tried to lay it on the serpent; and down to the present time men and women with one consent begin to make excuse.

Remember that these men Luke tells us about were not invited to a funeral, or to hear some dry, stupid lecture or sermon; they were not invited to visit a hospital, or a prison, or a madhouse; to witness some terrible scene or execution—something that would have pained them. It was to go to *a feast*.

The gospel is represented in the Bible as a feast. In the evening of this dispensation there is going to be the marriage supper of God's Son. Blessed is he that shall be at the marriage supper of the Lamb! If I know my own heart, I would rather be torn limb from limb, or have my heart taken from my body this moment, and be present on that glorious day, than have the wealth of the world rolled at my feet, and miss that wonderful banquet at the marriage of the Lamb.

Not only was this a feast, but it was *a royal feast*. If you had the honor of an invitation from the President—if you were invited to some great banquet, you would not hesitate to accept the invitation. You would want it to be put into the papers, to show how you had been honored. But here is something worth more than that. Here is an invitation from the King of kings, the Lord of lords, God's only Son. By and by He will take His bride into the bridal chamber. The marriage supper of the Lamb is hastening on. He has gone to prepare new mansions for His bride—the old mansions are not good enough; and He will come by-and-by and take her to Himself. It is an invitation to this feast that I bring you. The invitations are going out now to every corner of the earth. All are invited. For nearly nineteen hundred years God's messengers have been cro sing over valley and mountain, over desert and sea, from end to end of the earth, inviting men and women to the gospel feast. What an honor for worms of the dust!

When man prepares a feast, there is a great rush to see who will get the best place. But God prepares His feast, and the chairs would all be empty if His disciples did not go out and compel them to come in.

Then, when man prepares a feast, he invites his *friends*, those who love him; but God invites His *bitterest enemies*, those who are in rebellion against Him. And yet men make excuse! No sooner is the invitation given by God than the excuses begin to rain in.

Did you ever stop to think what would take place if God should take, at his word, every one who makes excuse?—if He were to say, " Yes if you want to be excused from this feast, I will excuse you," and with the next stroke should sweep them all from the face of the earth? Supposing every one in this land should be taken at their word, and laid in the arms of death, how many stores would be closed to-morrow, how many homes would be filled with mourning and tears? Not a saloonkeeper would be left to carry on his traffic; every rumseller wants to be excused. He knows that if he accepts this invitation, he would have to give up his hellish trade. He could not go on making fatherless children, and taking the bread out of the mouth of the orphan and the widow, and be going on his way to the marriage supper of the Lamb at the same time. Every saloonkeeper and every drunkard wants to be excused. If God *did* excuse them and take them away with a stroke, you would have no drunkards reeling through your streets. There would be no harlots then, for every harlot wants to be excused. She knows she has to give up her sins if she wants to be present at the supper of the Lamb. And your princely merchants, many of them, would be gone. They do not want to accept the invitation, because they think if they do they cannot make money so fast. They are carrying on some business which would then have to be stopped, and with one consent, they begin to make excuse. But oh, my friends, it would be a solemn time if God should take men at their word. The grass would soon be growing in the streets, and the living would be occupied in burying the dead.

Now, *be honest with God!* God is honest. He means what He says. This is an honest invitation, and He wants us to be honest. If you do not want to be at this supper, why not say so? Why make excuses? They are nothing but lies. If you can rise up and give a *reasonable* excuse—if so, tell us what it is—why you don't accept this invitation. *Think* for a minute. What valid reason can you give? You have none. It is not often we get an invitation to attend a royal feast, but here comes one to be present at the marriage supper of God's only Son. Is it not *downright folly* for any one to refuse? Just think what you are asking to be excused from. From heaven; from the society of the pure; from those who have washed their robes in the blood of the Lamb. Man asks to be excused from the mansions which Christ has prepared; from the society of the angels; from God the Father, and Christ the Son, and the Holy Ghost. All the really great men of the world are not down here, they are in heaven. You talk of the great men in England and America, but I tell you, the best this earth has ever had are there and the best that ever lived will be gathered at that feast. For six thousand years they have been gathering there— all the pure of the earth—Abraham, Isaac, and Jacob. Yes, we shall sit down with the patriarchs and prophets, the apostles and martyrs, with the best that have lived upon this earth.

I would rather die to-night and be sure of meeting the bliss of the purified in yon world of light, than live for centuries with the wealth of this world at my feet, and miss the marriage supper of the Lamb. I have missed many appointments in my life, but, by the grace of God, I mean to make sure of that one. Why, the blessed privilege of sitting down at the marriage supper of the Lamb, to see the King in His beauty, to be forever with the Lord—who would miss it?

Let us take up these three men, who "with one consent began to make excuse."

1. What did the first one say? "I have bought a piece of ground, and I must needs go and see it."

Some one has asked. Why did he not look at the ground before he bought it? If he had been a good business man, he would have seen his ground *first*. He couldn't make the bargain any better by going to look at it now, and now that he has got it, he can go and look at it at any time—the land could not run away! It was not that he had made a partial bargain and might withdraw, or that someone might step in ahead of him and get the ground from him. He did not even have that excuse. He had bought the land. There was no fear that he should lose his title to it. Yet he must needs go and see it. Strange time to go and see ground at supper-time!

On the face of it, it was a downright lie. He did not

want to go to the feast, and so he manufactured this excuse to ease his conscience. This is what the people make excuses for. The devil gets men into that cradle and rocks them to sleep in it.

2. What did the second man say? "I have bought five yoke of oxen, and I go to prove them. I pray thee have me excused."

Why not prove them before he bought them? It was no time to prove oxen after they were bought, and now that the bargain was closed he could prove them any time. Why not let them stand in the stall till he had accepted this invitation?

Don't you see that was another lie?

3. The third man's excuse was the most ridiculous of them all. "I have married a wife and therefore I cannot come."

Why did he not take his wife along with him? Who likes to go to a feast better than a young bride? He might have asked her to go too; and if she were not willing, then let her stay at home. The fact was, *he did not want to go.*

Eighteen hundred years have rolled away, and they tell us the world has grown wiser; they say it has improved wonderfully during these years; but tell me,

HAVE MEN GOT ANY BETTER EXCUSES?

Young lady! can you give a better excuse? Have you got an excuse that will stand the light of eternity, have you got an excuse that will even satisfy yourself? Men try every kind of excuse, but the man does not live who can give a good one. Let some terrible disease lay hold of a man, let death come and look him in the face, and his excuses are gone in a moment. My friend, your excuses will look altogether different when you come to stand before the great tribunal of your Judge.

I would just like to take up some of the popular excuses of the present day.

There is one very common one, "I do not like this minister or that preacher."

Well, what has that to do with it? What have you to do with *the messenger?* Suppose a boy comes and gives me a despatch, some good news from my wife. I don't turn round to see who brings it. He may be black or white, that is nothing to me. It is the message I care for. Is it not the fact that God invites you to a feast? What are you looking at the messenger for? I have heard this excuse till I am tired, "I don't like this minister or that minister, this person or that one who calls himself a Christian." Never mind about the *messenger.* The question is,

ARE YOU WILLING TO RECEIVE THE MESSAGE FROM GOD?

Do you believe the Word of God is true, and that God invites you to this feast? Do you believe that the invitation is to "every creature" in the world? You have nothing to do with the preacher who brings the message. If the message is from God, I ask you, why not accept it? If you are going to wait until you find some perfect man or woman to bring you the invitation, you will never accept it. There was never but one perfect Man. You will find a good many flaws in our character, a good many things you may not like in the followers of Christ, but I challenge you to find a flaw in the character of our Master. *He* bids you come. And any one who accepts the invitation He will receive.

Another excuse. "There are so many things I cannot understand."

No doubt about that. God says the carnal man cannot understand spiritual things, and the Bible is a spiritual book. How *can* the unregenerate heart understand the Bible?

"Well," you say, "if it is a sealed book, how am I going to be saved?"

Well, when God put salvation before the world, He put *that* very plain. The Word of God may be darkened to the natural man, but

THE WAY OF SALVATION IS WRITTEN SO PLAIN

that the little child of six years old can understand it if she will. Take this passage and see if you do not understand it:—"The Spirit and the bride say, Come; and let him that heareth say, Come; and let him that is athirst come." Are you not thirsty? God says—Come! "And whosoever will, let him take the water of life freely." You know what it is to take a gift? God puts salvation before you as a gift. "He came unto His own, and His own received Him not; but as many as received Him, to them gave He power to become the sons of God." You can understand that? "Believe on the Lord Jesus Christ and thou shalt be saved." You know what it is *to believe?* At any rate you know what it is to *trust,* to commit your soul to the Lord Jesus Christ—that is all.

There are dark and mysterious things in the Bible now, but when you begin to trust Christ your eyes will be opened, and the Bible will be a new book to you. Many things that are dark and mysterious to-day, to-morrow will have a new beauty. It will become the

Book of books to you. To-day Christ may be a root out of a dry ground, without form or comeliness, but He will become to you the chiefest among ten thousand, the altogether lovely, the bright and morning star, if you take Him as your Savior. Then you will understand the Bible.

No book in the world has been so misjudged as the Bible. Men judge it without reading it. Or perhaps they read a bit here and a bit there, and then close it, saying, "It is so dark and mysterious!" You take a book, now-a-days, and read it. Some one asks you what you think about it. "Well," you say, "I have only read it through once, not very carefully, and I should not like to give an opinion." Yet people take up God's Book, read a few pages, and condemn the whole of it. Of all the skeptics and infidels I have ever met speaking against the Bible, I have never met one who read it through. There may be such men, but I have never met them.

It is simply an excuse. There is no man living who will stand up before God and say that kept him out of the kingdom. It is the devil's work trying to make us believe it is not true, and that it is dark and mysterious. The only way to overcome the great enemy of souls is by the written Word of God. He knows that, and so tries to make men disbelieve it. As soon as a man is a true believer in the Word of God, he is a conqueror over Satan.

Young man! the Bible is true. What have infidels to give you in its place? What has made England but the open Bible? Every nation that exalteth the Word of God is exalted, and every nation that casteth it down is cast down. Oh, let us cling close to the Bible.

Of course, we shall not understand it all at once. But men are not to condemn it on that account. Suppose I should send my little boy, five years old, to school to-morrow morning, and when he came home in the afternoon I say to him, "Willie, can you read? can you write? can you spell? Do you understand all about algebra, geometry, Hebrew, Latin, and Greek?" "Why, papa," the little fellow would say, "how funny you talk; I have been all day trying to learn the A B C!" Suppose I should reply, "If you have not finished your education, you need not go any more"—what would you say? Why, you would say I had gone mad! There would be just as much reason in that as in the way people talk about the Bible.

My friends, the men who have studied the Bible for fifty years—the wise men and the scholars, the great theologians—have never got down to the depths of it yet. There are truths there that the Church of God has been searching out for the last eighteen hundred years, but no man has fathomed the depths of that ever-living stream.

There is another class who say, "That's not my difficulty. I believe the Word of God, but if I could speak to you alone, I would tell you my excuse. The fact is, I love the world very much, and if I become a Christian, I shall have to give up all pleasure, and go through the world with a long face, and never smile again. My joy will be forever gone!"

I want to say here that no greater lie was ever forged than that. The devil started it away back in Eden, but there is not one word of truth in it; it is

A LIBEL UPON CHRISTIANITY.

It does *not* make a man gloomy to become a child of God.

See! there is a man going to execution. In a few moments he will be launched into eternity. But, flashing over the wires, comes a message from the President. He sends a reprieve. I run in haste to the man. I shout, "Good news! good news! You are *not* to die!" Does that make him gloomy? No! no! no!

Young men, young women, old and young, don't believe Satan's lies any longer. It is the *want* of Christ that makes men gloomy. Take a man who is really thirsty, dying for want of water, and go and give him water. Is that going to make him gloomy? That is what Christ is—water to the thirsty soul. If a man is dying for want of bread, and you give him bread, is that to make him gloomy? That is what Christ is to the soul—the bread of life. You will never have true pleasure or peace or joy or comfort until you have found Christ.

Another excuse—how thick they are! The air is full of them. I hear some one say, " Well, I should like to be a Christian, but *it is a very hard thing*. I have tried it a good many times. I would not like to speak right out, but that is just the honest truth."

I will tell you what you have been doing—you have been trying to serve God with the old carnal mind. You might as well try to walk to the moon! It is utterly impossible. The Ethiopian cannot change his skin; the leopard cannot change its spots. It is impossible to serve God with the old carnal heart; but with the new heart God will give you the power, and you will not then be talking about its being hard to serve Him. That is just

ANOTHER LIE.

Let us look at it.

Do you mean to say that God is a hard Master? Do you say it is a hard thing to serve God, and do you say that Satan is an easy master, and that it is easier to serve him than God? Is it honest—is it true? God a hard master! If I read my Bible right, I read *that the way of the transgressor is hard.* Let me tell you it is the devil that who is the hard master. Yes, "The way of the transgressor is hard." The Word of God cannot be changed. If you doubt it, young man, look at the convict in the prison, right in the bloom of manhood, right in the prime of life. He has been there for ten years, and must remain for ten years more—twenty years taken out of his life, and when he comes out of that miserable cell, he comes out a branded felon! Do you think *that* man will tell you "The way of the transgressor has been easy"? Go ask the poor drunkard, this man who is bound hand and foot, the slave of the infernal cup, who is hastening onwards to a drunkard's hell. Ask him if he has found the way of the transgressor easy. "Easy?" he will cry—"Easy? The way of the transgressor is hard and gets harder and harder every day!" Go ask the libertine and the worldling, go ask the gambler and the blasphemer—with one voice they will tell you that the service has been hard. Take the most faithful follower of the devil and put questions to him.

The best way to settle this matter is to find out by the testimony of those that have served both masters. I do not think a man has any right to judge until he has served both. If I heard a man condemn a master, I should be very apt to ask if he had served him; and if he had not, he could not very well testify. Now, if you have served two masters, then you are very good judges.

I want to stand as a witness for Christ. I have been in this school for forty years, and I want to testify that I have found him an easy master. I used to say, as you do, "It is a hard thing to be a Christian," and I thought it was; but now I tell you that the yoke is easy and the burden light. And I am speaking to many more who have served both masters. Many of you have served Christ, and many of you, before you were brought into His fold, served the devil. I would like to ask you, you that are Christ's, you who have served Him—some five, some ten, some twenty years—is Jesus a hard master? I have never heard a man say, "I have served Christ for five years, or for ten, and found Him a hard master." And now let me put you into the witness-box again. For many years you served Satan; did you not find him a hard master? O yes! my friends you cannot help admitting it, you *know* it is true. *The way of the transgressor is hard.*

Suppose we could go beyond this life; suppose we could go down to the bottomless pit, and summon up Judas, who has been there for nearly nineteen hundred years. Suppose we put the question to him, "Judas, you betrayed the Son of God, sold Him for thirty pieces of silver. You have served the devil faithfully. Have you found his service an easy one?" What a wail would rise from those lips! Do you think Judas found it easy? Do you think he found Satan a kind master? See him throwing down the thirty pieces of silver! Why, he got so tired of the devil's service that he hanged himself twenty-four hours after publicly entering it.

Now let us call upon Paul who, you may say, took
the place that Judas once filled. Let him come down
from the hilltops of glory. Do you think he would say
it was a hard thing to serve God, and an easy thing to
serve the devil? "I served the devil well," he says,
"I breathed out threatenings, I persecuted the Church.
But *it was hard for me to kick against the pricks.*"

And now let us see what God says about it. I would
like to ask those who think Him a hard master, what
they would do with a passage like this, " Come unto me,
all ye that labor and are heavy-laden, and I will give
you rest. Take my yoke upon you and learn of me;
for I am meek and lowly in heart, and ye shall find rest
unto your souls. *For my yoke is easy,* and my burden
is light" ? Yes, it is an easy thing to serve anyone we
love. If you love a person how you delight to please
them.

Oh, my friend, do not dishonor God by calling Him
a hard master.

I beg of you, do not listen to Satan's lies. He has
deceived the whole human race. Oh, will you not
change masters now, and accept the invitation to be
present at the marriage supper of the Lamb?

EXCUSES.

PART II.

The next excuse I want to take up is "election." I meet a great many in the inquiry-room who tell me they are very anxious to be saved, but they do not know if they are elected. "If I were only sure that I were elected," they say, "I would soon be in earnest about salvation. But then I don't know that I'm one of the elect, so I have a very good excuse."

Now, I want to give no uncertain sound upon this point. I want to say that an unconverted person has nothing whatever to do with the doctrine of election. After you have become children of God, then we can talk about election—then we can consider how sweet and beautiful the doctrine is. But those who are not God's children have nothing at all to do with it. You do not like any one else to read your private letters, do you? Well, the doctrine of election was

WRITTEN IN A PRIVATE LETTER

to the children of God. No wonder the world puzzles over it. No wonder they cannot understand it. It was never meant for them. What they have to do with is the "Whosoever" and the "Him that cometh" of the free invitations of Christ.

Suppose I am taking a walk near this hall to-night, and say to the policeman at the door, "Who is invited to this meeting?" "Those who have tickets," he replies. I have no ticket, so it is not for me. I walk on further, and come to another meeting. "This is only for those belonging to the ——— Society," I am told, so I know it is not for me. I go on further, and come to a large public building—a club. "Only members admitted," I read on the door. It is not for me either. I go further still and come to another building and over the door this is written: "Whosoever will, let him come in." Ah! it is for me this time. "Whosoever"—that means me—and in I go. My friend, God puts it just like that. All are invited to come to Christ. What have you to do with Paul's epistle about election? You have nothing to do with it—not till you become a Christian. You have no business with the private letters of other people, and the "whosoever" comes before election. If you learn to read, you commence with the alphabet, don't you? You don't learn to read all at once. And if you come to Christ you must come in God's way; and then you can talk about how you came.

"Yes, but," you say, "there is another side to that. Christ said, 'No man can come to me except the Father, which hath sent me, draw him.'"

Well, I say Christ *is* drawing men. "I, if I be lifted up, will draw all men unto me." He is drawing men, but they will not come. God was in Christ reconciling the world unto Himself, and drawing men unto Him. That drawing is going on now, but many a heart is fighting against the strivings of the Spirit. God is drawing men heavenward, and the devil is drawing them hellward.

Supposing a man, wishing to go to New York, should say, "I don't know if God has decreed it. If I am to be there, I will be there. Anyhow, it is no use my taking the train. What is the use of my paying the fare and taking trouble about it? If I am elected to get there I will get there somehow." Who would use such language as that? Or, suppose a farmer were to say, ' I am not going to plant. If God has decreed that I am to have a crop, I shall have it. I am not going to trouble myself tilling the ground or working hard. If God has decreed that I will have a good harvest, why, I shall have it without any tilling." Or, suppose you are sick, and do not send for a doctor. Suppose you say, " If God has decreed it, I shall get well," so you refuse to take the medicines. You say, "There is no use in it. If God has decreed that I am to get well, I will get well without it." Who ever talks in that way? Yet a good many people carry out that very doctrine with re-gard to spiritual things.

I have an idea that the Lord Jesus saw how men were going to stumble over this doctrine, so after He had been thirty or forty years in heaven; He came down and spoke to John. One Lord's=day in Patmos, He said to him, " Write these things to the churches." John kept on writing. His pen flew very fast. And then the Lord, when it was nearly finished, said, " John, before you close the book, put this in: 'The Spirit and the Bible say, Come; and let him that heareth say, Come.' But there will be some that are deaf, and they cannot hear, so add, 'Let him that is athirst, Come'; and in case there should be any that do not thirst, put it still broader, ' *Whosoever will*, let him take of the water of life freely.'" What more can you have than that? The Book is *sealed*, as it were, with that. It is the last in-vitation in the Bible. "Whosoever will, let him take of the water of life freely." You are thirsty. You want

water. I hold out this glass to you, and say, "Take it."
You say, "If I am decreed to have it, I am not going to
put myself to the trouble of taking it." Well, you will
never get it. And if you are ever to have salvation, you
must reach out the hand and take it. "I will take the
cup of salvation, and call upon the name of the Lord."
Will you take it now? It is simple enough; it is a gift.
"The wages of sin is death, but *the gift of God* is eternal life."

My dear friend, do not stumble over the doctrine of
election any longer. You will not be able to stand up
before God and say, "I did not accept the invitation
because I was not one of the elect." That excuse will
fade away in His presence. God invites every man and
woman to the gospel feast when He writes, "Whosoever
will, let him take."

I can imagine there is a man who says, "That is not
my difficulty. I know a man who belongs to the professing Church of Christ, and he cheated me out of five
dollars some years ago. There are

HYPOCRITES IN THE CHURCH,

and I am not going to have anything to do with it. No!
you don't catch me going into company with hypocrites."

Well, I will find you two hypocrites in the world for
every one you will find in the Church. Besides, I am
not asking you to come to the Church—not but that I
believe in the Church—but I am asking you to the
marriage supper of the Lamb. Come to Christ first,
and then we can talk to you about the Church There
always have been hypocrites in the Church and always
will be. One of the twelve apostles turned out to be a

hypocrite, and there will be hypocrites in the Church to the end of time. But there will not be one hypocrite at this feast, and if you want to get out of the company of hypocrites you had better make haste and come to Christ. If you do not accept the invitation you will have to spend eternity with them. Suppose every professing Christian were a black-hearted hypocrite, what has that to do with you? "Follow *thou* me," says Christ. You are not to be looking to John, or Peter, or Paul, this man or that, but straight to Christ. You may find many flaws in our characters, but you will find none in Christ's. We find a good many in ourselves and you may too. But we do not ask you to follow us, but Christ. There will be no hypocrites at the marriage supper of the Lamb; they will all be in the lost world. And if you do not accept the invitation you will have to spend eternity with hypocrites. So if you really object to them, you had better make sure of a place at the marriage supper of the Lamb.

But a self-righteous Pharisee says, "Well, I don't understand all this talk about conversion; I'm

GOOD ENOUGH AS I AM.

My excuse will stand if the others won't. I am not going into that inquiry-room to talk with these people, and beg them to pray for me. I don't need it." And he draws his filthy rags of self-righteousness about him and thinks he is pure in the sight of God and man.

My friend, the Word of God says, "There is none righteous, no not one." If you are found with your own garment on, you will be cast out from this feast. He will furnish you with a robe of spotless white if you will accept it, but you need not think you can stand in the presence of the King with these miserable rags of self righteousness about you.

Oh, may the Holy Spirit show you how vile you are in the sight of a holy God! The nearer a man gets to God, the more he abhors himself. You know when a man is getting near is God, he begins to loathe himself Like Job, he says, "I abhor myself." Like Isaiah, when he saw the holy God, he cries out, "Woe is me, I am undone." Like that holy man Daniel, his comeliness is turned to corruption. May God strip you of your self=righteousness to=day!

But here is another excuse. If the devil cannot make a man believe he is good enough without being saved, then he will tell him he is so bad the Lord will have nothing to do with him. A great many have that excuse. "I would like to be saved," they say, " but I am

TOO BAD."

That is another lie. Why, what does the Scripture say? "Christ died for the ungodly." Jesus Christ came into the world to save sinners. What did Christ say to His disciples? "Go ye into all the world and preach the gospel *to every creature*." "That repentance and remission of sins should be preached in His name *among all nations, beginning at Jerusalem*." The very men whose hands were dripping with the blood of the Son of God, had salvation offered to them! Paul said he was the *chief of sinners*, and if he was saved, surely there is hope for every man on the face of the earth.

If you are so bad, you are the very one He wants to save. During our war, I remember the doctor used to go after a battle to look at the wounded men, and he would find out the most desperate cases and attend to them first. That is the way the great Physician does now. He saves the worst men He can get. I know a great many people who are anxious to come, but they are waiting until they grow a little better. They think God will not take them till then.

Now, notice, my friend, the Lord invites you to come just as you are, and if you could make yourself better you would not be any more acceptable to Him. Do not put these filthy rags of self-righteousness about you. God will strip every rag from you when you come to Him, and clothe you with glorious garments. When the war was going on, we would sometimes go to the recruiting office and see a man come in with a silk hat, broadcloth coat, calfskin boots— his suit might be worth $100; and another man would come in whose clothes were not worth a dollar; but they both had to strip and put on the uniform of the country. And so when we go into Christ's vineyard we must put on the livery of heaven and be stripped of every rag. So, however bad you are, come just as you are, and the Lord will receive you.

I have read of an artist who wanted to paint a picture of the Prodigal Son. He searched through the madhouses and the poorhouses and the prisons to find a man wretched enough to represent the prodigal, but he could not find one. One day he was walking down the street and met a man who he thought would do. He told the poor beggar he would pay him well if he came to his room and sat for his portrait. The beggar agreed, and the day was appointed for him to come. The day came, and a man put in his appearance at the artist's room. "You made an appointment with me," he said, when he was shown into the studio. The artist looked at him. "I never saw you before," he said; "You cannot have an appointment with me." "Yes," he said, "I agreed to meet you to-day at ten o'clock." "You must be mistaken. It must have been some other artist. I was to see a *beggar* here at this hour." "Well," said the beggar, "I am he." "You?" "Yes." "Why, what have you been doing?" "Well, I thought I would dress myself up a bit before I got painted." "Then," said the artist, "I do not want you. I wanted you *as you were*. *Now* you are no use to me."

That is the way Christ wants every poor sinner, just as he is. I think I can hear someone say, "Oh, but my heart is so hard." Well, that is just the very reason you ought to come. If you had not a hard heart you would not need a Savior. Do you think you can soften your heart? Can you break your heart? Did not God invite the hard-hearted? Did not Christ come to seek and to save that which was lost? It is just because men's hearts are hard that they need a Savior. So that is no excuse at all. God invites you, and you cannot stand up and say to the Great King you did not accept the invitation because you had a hard heart. He invites "whosoever," and you can come along with your hard heart just as it is.

Then comes another excuse "I should like to come, but somehow or other I do not know that I feel just right." That is

A VERY COMMON EXCUSE—

Feeling, feeling, feeling, feeling! I have heard that cry till I am sick of it.

Suppose a friend invites me to dinner to-day, and I say, "Well, I would like very much to take dinner with you. There is no man I would rather dine with than yourself; but I do not know that I *feel* just right." " Are you sick?" he might ask. "No, I never felt better in my life." " Well, what do you mean?" "I don't know that I *feel* just right. I do not know that I will be in a right state of mind." "I do not understand you," he would say; "what do you mean?" "Well, I would like to go very much, but I don't feel right."

That is the way men are talking now. " I would like to go to heaven, but I don't know that I have got the right kind of feeling." But, my friend, if you really want to, God invites you, and that is all about it. My friend urges me to come, but I keep on saying, "I do not know that I am in the right state of mind." "Why," he would say, "I think Mr. Moody must have gone out of his mind. I invited him to dinner, and instead of giving me a plain answer he kept talking about feeling all the time!" You may smile at it, but that is just the way people talk in the inquiry-room—hundreds of them.

My friend, does God invite you? If He does, why don't you accept the invitation? If you want to come, just come along, and don't be talking about feeling. Do you think Lazarus had any feeling when Christ called him out of the sepulcher?

God is above feeling. Do you think you can control your feelings? I am sure if I could control my feelings I never would have any bad feelings, I would always have good feelings. But bear in mind Satan may change our feelings fifty times a day, but he cannot change the Word of God; and what we want is to build our hopes of heaven upon the Word of God. When a poor sinner is coming up out of the pit, and just ready to get his feet upon the Rock of Ages, the devil sticks out a plank of feeling, and says, "Get on that," and when he puts his feet on that, down he goes again. Take one of these texts—"Verily, I say unto you, he that heareth my word and believeth on Him that sent me *hath* everlasting life, and *shall not* come into condemnation, but *is passed* from death unto life." My friend, that is worth more than all the feelings that you can have in a whole lifetime. I would a thousand times rather stand on that verse than on all the frames and feelings I ever had. I took my stand there forty years ago. Since then the dark waves of hell have come dashing up against me, the waves of persecution have broken all around me; doubts, fears, and unbelief in turn have assailed me; but I have been able to stand firm on this short Word of God. It is a sure footing for eternity. It was true 1900 years ago, and it is true to-day. That rock is higher than my feeling, and what we need is to get our feet upon the rock, and the Lord will put a new song in our mouths.

But I hear some one say, "He has not touched my case at all. None of these things ever trouble me; but the fact is

I CANNOT BELIEVE.

I would like to come, but I cannot believe."

Not long ago a man said to me, "I cannot believe." "*Whom?*" I asked. He stammered and said again, "I cannot believe." I said, "*Whom?*" "Well," he said, "I *can't* believe." "Whom?" I asked again. At last he said, "I cannot believe myself." Well, you don't need to. You do not need to put any confidence in yourself. The less you believe in yourself the better. But if you tell me you can't believe God, that is another thing; and I would like to ask you why!" If a man says to me, "I have a great respect for you; I have a great admiration for you; but I do not believe a word you say," I say to myself, "I certainly do not think much of your admiration." But that is the way a good many people talk about God. They say, "I have a profound reverence for God; the very name of God strikes awe to my heart; but I do not believe Him." Why don't you be honest and say at once you *won't* believe?

There is no real reason why men cannot believe God. I challenge any infidel on the face of the earth to put his finger on one promise God has ever made that He has not kept. The idea of a man standing up in the evening of the nineteenth century and saying he cannot believe God! My friend, you have no reason for not be lieving Him. If you say you cannot believe man there would be some reason in that, because men very often say what is not true. But God never makes any mistakes. "Has He said it and shall He not make it good?" Believe in God and say as Job says: "Though He slay me, yet will I trust Him."

Some men talk as if it were a great misfortune that they do not believe. They seem to look upon it as a kind of infirmity, and think they ought to be sympathized with and pitied. But bear in mind that it is

THE MOST DAMNING SIN OF THE WORLD.

"When He (the Holy Ghost) is come, He will reprove the world of sin, and of righteousness, and of judgment: of sin, *because they believe not on me*." That is the sin of the world—"they believe not on me." That is the very root of sin; and the fruit is bad, for the tree is bad.

May God open our eyes to see that He is true, and may we all be led to put our fullest trust in Christ!

But here is another one who says, "I would like to come very much, but *I am*

AFRAID I WOULD NOT HOLD OUT."

Now, I have had a rule for a number of years that has been a help to me—never to cross a mountain until I come to it. You trust Christ to save you now. The devil throws a little straw across your path, and then tries to magnify it and makes you think it is a great mountain. Never mind the mountains; trust Him to save you now. If He can save you to-day He can keep you to-morrow. When you have sat down at the banquet and had one good feast—when you have had one interview with Christ, you will not want to leave Him. I accepted this invitation forty years ago, and I have never wanted to go back. I have not had to keep myself all these years. I would have been back in twenty-four hours if I had. Thank God, we do not have to keep ourselves. The Lord is my Keeper—my Shepherd, I shall not want. He keeps us. It takes the same grace to keep us that it does to save us, and God has told us that His grace is sufficient for us.

But some people are not at all afraid of falling away. They are sure that God is quite able to save them, and quite strong enough to keep them. But when you ask them if they are Christians, they say, "Well, you know, *I would like to be, but*

I HAVE NO TIME."

If I were to take you by the hand and say, "My friend, why not accept of the invitation now?" you might say, "Please excuse me at present. I have really no time,

I have got some very pressing business to attend to to-morrow morning, and I have to go home as fast as possible to get my night's rest. You must really excuse me." And the mothers would say, "We have to run home and put the children to bed. You must excuse us this time." So thousands and thousands say they have no time to be religious.

But, my friend, what have you done with all the time that God has given you? What have you been doing all these months and years that have rolled away since He gave you birth? Is it true you have no time? What did you do with the 365 days of last year? Had you no time during all these twelve months to seek the Kingdom of God? You spend *twenty years* getting an education to enable you to earn a living for this poor frail body, so soon to be eaten up of worms. You spend *seven or eight years* in learning a trade, that you may earn your daily bread. And yet you have not *five minutes* to accept this invitation of Christ's! My friend, bear in mind you have yet to find time to die, to stand in the presence of the Judge; and when He calls you to stand before that bar, will you dare to tell Him that you had no time to prepare for the marriage supper of His Son?

You have no time? Take time! Let everything else be laid aside until you have accepted this invitation. Do you not know that it is a lie? If you have not time, take it. "Seek *first* the Kingdom of God." Let your business be suspended to-morrow. Suppose you do not get so much money to-morrow. What matters it if you get Christ? Better for a man to be sure of salvation than to "gain the whole world and lose his own soul."

But you say "I would like to become a Christian, but I have

A PREJUDICE

against these special meetings, and against evangelists, and against a layman too. If it was a regular minister, if it was our regular minister, I would accept the invitation."

If that is your difficulty, I can help you out of it. You can walk straight over to your minister, and have a talk with him. And if you say you do not want to be converted in a special meeting, there are regular meetings in all the churches, and your minister would be heartily glad to talk with you about your soul.

But if you say, "There is a great awakening here in this city, and I do not like to be converted in the time of a revival," you can step into a train, and go to some town where there is no revival. We can find you some place where there is no revival, and some church where there is not much of the revival spirit, without very much difficulty. If you really want to go, pray don't give that for an excuse.

How wise the devil is! When the church is cold, and everything is dead, men say, "Oh, well, if there was only some life in the church I might become a Christian. If we could only just have a wave of blessing from heaven, it could be so easy then." Then when the wave does come they say, "Oh, no, we are afraid of excitement, and afraid of these special meetings. We are afraid something will be done that won't be just in accordance with our ideas of propriety."

Oh, my friends, do not listen to these subtle lies. Just come as you are to Christ, and accept the offer which He makes you now!

I wish I had time to go on with these excuses, but

they are as numerous as the hairs of my head; and if I could go on, and tried to exhaust them all, the devil would help people to make more. The best thing you can do is to tie them all into one bundle, and stamp them as a pack of lies; not a single one of them is true. God will sweep them all away some day if you do not do it now.

It is a very solemn thought that God will excuse you if you want to be excused. He does not wish to do it, but He *will* do it. "As I live, saith the Lord, I have no pleasure in the death of the wicked; but that the wicked turn from his way and live. Turn ye, turn ye from your evil ways; for why will ye die, O house of Israel!" Look at the Jewish nation. They wanted to be excused from the feast. They despised the grace of God and trampled it under foot, and look at them to-day! Yes, it is easy enough to say, "I pray Thee have me excused," but by-and-by God may take you at your word, and say, "Yes, I will excuse you." And in that lost world, while others who have accepted the invitation sit down to the marriage supper of the Lamb amid shouts and hallelujahs in heaven, you will be crying in the company of the lost, "The harvest is past, the summer is ended, and we are not saved."

And remember, it is the King of kings, the Lord of glory, who invites you to this feast. Come just as you are, and accept the invitation. Let the plow stand in the furrow until you have accepted it. Let the store be closed till then; let business be suspended until you have accepted it. Let the land rest; yes, let the ox stand in the stall, until you have accepted that invitation. Make sure, whatever you do, that you will not be missing from the marriage supper of the Lamb. That sainted mother of yours will be there. That little child who died a few months ago will be there.

Young lady! do you want to be excused? He will excuse you. Do you want to be excused, young man? He will excuse you. You may make light of it now, if choose. "Oh no," you say, "I never do that. Whatever I have been guilty of, I have never done that!" Have you not? Suppose I get an invitation to dinner to-morrow; I take it and tear it up; I do not answer it; I pay no attention to it. Is not that making light of it? How many of you will go away to-night paying no attention to this invitation? Every one who goes home in a careless spirit, is he not making light of it? The Lord has invited you to the gospel feast. Are you going to accept or make light of the invitation? God does not want you to die; He wants you to accept this invitation and live.

If you have a good excuse, one that will stand the light of eternity, hold on to it. Do not give it up for anything. Take it down with you into the grave. Hold it firm, take it to the bar of God, and tell it out to Him. But if you have not got one that will not stand the test of eternity, give it up. If you have an excuse that will not stand the piercing eye of God, I beg of you as a friend, give it up now. Let it go to the four winds of heaven, and accept the invitation to be at the marriage supper of the Lamb. Do not let the laughing, scoffing, mocking world laugh your soul into eternal death. Do as the pilgrim whom John Bunyan describes, who started out from the City of Destruction, crying, "Life, life, eternal life!" Set your face like a flint towards that Blessed Land, and say, "By the grace of God, I will be at the marriage supper of the Lamb."

Suppose we should write out to-night this excuse. How would it sound? " *To the King of Heaven. While sitting in the —— Hall, City of ——, July —, 18—, I received a very pressing invitation from one of your servants to be present at the marriage supper of your only-begotten Son.* I PRAY THEE HAVE ME EXCUSED."

Would you sign that, young man? Would you, mother? Would you come up to the reporter's table, take up a pen and put your name down to such an excuse? You would say, " Let my right hand forget its cunning, and my tongue cleave to the roof of my mouth before I sign that." I doubt if there is one here who would sign it. Will you then pay no attention to God's invitation? I beg of you do not make light of it. It is a loving God inviting you to a feast, and God is not to be mocked. Go play with the forked lightning, go trifle with pestilence and disease, but trifle not with God.

Just let me write out another answer. " *To the King of Heaven. While sitting in the —— Hall, July—, 18—, I received a pressing invitation from one of your messengers to be present at the marriage supper of your only-begotten Son. I hasten to reply.* BY THE GRACE OF GOD I WILL BE PRESENT."

Who will sign that? Is there one who will put his name to it? Is there no one who will say, " By the grace of God I will accept the invitation now " ? May God bring you to a decision now. If you would ever see the kingdom of God, you must decide this question one way or the other. What will you do with the invitation? I bring it to you in the name of my Master; will you accept or reject it? Be wise to-night, and accept the invitation. Make up your mind you will not go away till the question of eternity is settled.